Forbidden Psychology 101

How To Use Psychology To influence Human Behavior And Read People (UNKNOWINGLY)

Table of Contents

Introduction 1

Chapter One: Why We Want to Be Liked 25

Chapter Two: Being Likable by Not Being Unlikable.................... 44

Chapter Three: The Confidence Machine 70

Chapter Four: Learning New Skills.................... 74

Chapter Five: How Other People See You 90

Chapter Six: Humour and Likability 114

Chapter Seven: Communication.................... 121

Chapter Eight: Starting Conversations 141

Chapter Nine: Meeting People 163

Chapter Ten: How to Act Around Strangers 169

Chapter Eleven: Dating 186

Chapter Twelve: How to Make Friends and Keep Them 206

Chapter Thirteen: Putting it all to Good Use 220

Final Thoughts 232

Introduction

"Our lives improve only when we take chances – and the first and most difficult risk we can take is to be honest with ourselves."

– Walter Anderson, Editor, Parade Magazine

Hi, I'm Mark Williams and firstly I'd like to say a big thank you for purchasing The Likeability Blueprint.

Many hundreds of hours has gone into research and writing of this, and I did it because I want to make a difference and to make your life better.

I wasn't always a well respected success coach, or likeability specialist. Actually the reason why I know so much about this stuff, and how to make YOUR life better as a result of it, is all because I used to be such an unconfident introvert.

That experience for over half my life, of being bullied in school... Of having to work really hard to get people's respect in adulthood, struggles with my relationships, and with my struggles to get myself noticed at work, and to make new friendships... All of that struggle really was a gift.

It was a gift because it gave me the opportunity to learn and appreciate the power of Auto Magnetism and to be able to share it with you in this book.

Don't get me wrong I did have a few close friends...who have stuck by me through thick and thin over the years.

But what I've gained is more than just a large number of friends... It's an aura of respect and personal magnetism that follows me wherever I go.

My opinion gets respected at work, my wife respects me and what I have to say, and my friends and colleagues look up to me.

And I want that to happen to you. Honestly the world is a super amazing place and it looks a whole lot better when you have Auto-Magnetism that I'm going to share with you.

Firstly, please read the quote that I've just shared with you at the top of this page, from Walter Anderson. I shared it because it's super important.

Honestly, the greatest things in life come from stepping slightly outside your comfort zone, and sometimes on this journey you might just have to be honest with yourself and realize that in order to change for the better, you might need to take a chance with what I have to share with you.

So, what I'm saying is... If you are serious about becoming more successful in life... ...If you're serious about becoming a person who exudes personal charm and charisma... Then you need to take ACTION with what you learn in this book.

Up until now, any lack of respect anyone has shown you, any lack of ability at forming friendships, any difficulty getting your opinion across at work... None of this has been your fault.

You did the best that you could with what you know.

And this is the journey that you were meant to be on. Accept it, embrace it, love yourself as you are RIGHT HERE, RIGHT NOW. Because in order for other people to love you, you have to love yourself as you are right now.

When I started training myself in Auto-Magnetism, I started off with a couple of affirmations.

I used affirmations because they are a great way to reprogram your brain to take on a new belief system.

It's like dropping a drop of red dye into a bucket every day. Sooner or later that bucket will turn red.

The same is true with affirmations (or meditation if that is better for you). With affirmations you just say the same thing over and over again for 5 minutes a day, every day, for 60-90 days. Until you've imprinted a new belief or habit upon your brain.

So I started with these two affirmations... "I love the way I am" And "I'm genuinely interested in other people"

What was really important about doing the affirmations was that I transferred these beliefs to my subconscious mind. So that even when my mind is wandering, at a split seconds notice, my brain just naturally operates this way now.

I DO love myself and accept myself as I am right here, right now.

And I AM genuinely interested in other people at a subconscious level. I'm not trying to manipulate people by asking them questions about themselves, or by joking around with them about something funny they just did...

...All that just naturally came by rewiring my brain to think that way at all times. Even when I'm not aware I'm doing it.

Other affirmations I've used on myself include "I'm supremely self-confident and I love taking risks" and "Every day in every way I'm getting better, better and better" Now the fact that in a relatively short space of time I turned my whole life around for the better, and have achieved permanent change in my whole life outlook, proves something very important...

Likability is not a genetic trait.

This is very important because I used to just think that I was born with low social skills. But the fact that I've been able to totally not only improve my social skills but become the kind of person who people GRAVITATE to, has proven to me

that this stuff can be learned and it's my mission to share it with you.

No one is born as the next President of the United States. Not everyone is a future movie star or Fortune 500 CEO from birth.

You know that nerdy guy from high school who shows up at the reunion with a $1000 suit and a super model wife?

That's a guy who perhaps was never innately likable – he learned how to do it. He learned what people want to hear and see and then delivered it with precision.

He learned how to make a killer first impression, and then keep it going day after day. You can do the same thing.

You just need to sit back, relax and take a good hard look at what people like in other people and what's holding you back.

Take, for example, pre-schoolers in a 1992 study conducted at George Mason University. The study set out to determine if pre-schoolers were likable based on earlier likability or pro-social activity.

In short, does a child with minimal world experience have an innately likable nature or is it affected by being around other people and being introduced to likable traits? It's the classic nature vs. nurture argument, and guess what?

This study, along with a dozen of others point overwhelmingly to the fact that they were likable because they were social – not because they were born likable.

Like a Moth to a Flame

Have you ever wondered why some people seem to be popular no matter where they go, as if they born that way?

It's like they have a magnetizing kind of energy that draws people of both sexes to them on.

The secret isn't in the clothes they wear, or the size of the waistline. In fact, it's in something called the secret auto-magnetism.

Auto-magnetism encompasses many different traits—traits you may already possess but fail to show off to others—even though it exists. Secret auto-magnetism is a set of traits (see below) that naturally, organically and positively bring people to you.

Think about your supervisor that never seems to notice your work, no matter how hard you work.

Or, that guy or girl you've had your eye on or months now, but who continually passes you up for somebody else—and you can't seem to figure out why.

The secret is...you're not flipping the auto-magnetism switch...a switch that when activated, will allow others to be drawn to you like a moth to a flame.

The traits are:

- Positivity
- Kindness
- Empathy
- Compassion
- Fun loving nature
- Confidence
- Sincerity
- Good listener

Becoming a master at body language (and learning how to read other's body language). Have you ever met someone who seems to go out of his or her way to become well liked? It can be a little painful to watch.

Someone that is 'trying too hard' is like watching a train wreck. You know what's coming—a rejection by his peers or his subordinates—but you just can't stop that train from coming. What most people fail to realize is that you don't have to spend time and money wining and dining people to like you. You don't have to act in a way that's not in line with who you are. You don't have to change anything about yourself—but instead, simply learn how to bring out your best self to others... ...by showing them you are a confident, empathetic, sincere, kind and fun loving individual.

People gravitate towards others who make them feel good, and in my experience, showing people who I am at my core, by being the fun loving, joyful person I am is exactly what has scored me date after date, job after job, and opportunity after opportunity (in every capacity of my life).

The shoe switch method is one of the first techniques I developed for this program, and it's perfect for a beginner, or anyone who may be feeling timid about getting started. The shoe switch method is simple.

All you have to do is pick three people that you admire, and then notice how much you have in common with them!

Let's say you admire Kobe Bryant (former L.A. Lakers player), Robin Williams (now deceased comedian and actor) and Oprah. Watch their movies, games, and TV shows. Write down as many personality traits as you can.

What similarities do you hold?

Robin Williams is funny, but so are you! Oprah is empathetic, and so are you, etc. Make an ongoing list of every trait you notice and tape it on your refrigerator door or desktop screen at work.

Being likeable doesn't have to do with anything but utilizing the secret auto-magnetism.

The results are radical, because any time you are honest about who you are, loving, positive and kind, that's just a magnetizing kind of energy that draws people in, and opens up doors for you that you've never had before.

You'll learn many different techniques for applying the secret auto-magnetism into your life, but here's just a snapshot as to what it can for you, immediately after you begin using it:

- Your inbox will be flooded with invites to parties, happy hours with co-workers who never before gave you the time of day, and gorgeous strangers you used to only admire from afar.
- You'll become an expert interviewer—just imagine being able to conquer any interview for any job you want (and get it on the spot!)
- Conversations with difficult people aren't easy—but likeable people are easily able to persuade others to do what they ask (even the most difficult people in your life will jump on board.)
- Your social life will radically expand—everyone wants to be around likeable people

Likability is a learned trait and I'm here to tell you that you can get there a lot quicker and a lot easier than you think. But, first let me tell you a bit about how this book works.

A lot of books are written as "definitive" guides to X, Y, or Z.

You start at point A and keep reading until you reach Z and beyond. But, in the Likability Blueprint, you're going to find that a lot of the tips and strategies I outline for you will reference back to previous chapters and exercises.

I didn't write this book in a linear fashion, nor should you necessarily use it in one.

Here's what I recommend: read the entire book straight through and let your brain absorb everything it has to offer.

You'll be shocked to know just how much your brain can do on its own (more in Chapter 2).

Once you've done that, go back through to chapters as you need to and take a closer look at the tips that can help you grow more confident, approach new people, and generate the social life you've always dreamed of.

And to put it all together, I've included a handful of exercises and introspective questions for you to work through with every chapter.

If you're unsure about any of the strategies or points I've outlined, dive headfirst into the content and read more about what you can do with it in these exercise sections.

Throughout the book I'm going to use the word "relationship" a lot. For some of you, it's a loaded term – you think of romance and time together in a quiet atmosphere.

But, what I mean is something more general; the overarching relationships you have with family and friends in addition to your love life. So, when you see relationship, think of it in as broad of terms as possible. I'll specify when I mean it to be a romantic relationship.

Who Should Be Reading This?

"By yourself. Everyone else is already taken."

– Oscar Wilde

I remember the first time that I felt out of the social circle, and well, not well liked—and it was traumatic.

It actually set me back for years, feeling like I just didn't have what it took to be liked by my peers. I remember the moment it happened like it was yesterday.

It was in the fourth grade.

That afternoon that I left school everything was normal, fine.

We were all friends.

Then, the next day I had to stay home from school because I wasn't feeling well and when I returned to school the day after that, cliques had formed.

There were friends of mine who no longer played with me during recess, or wanted to be my art buddy—and there were others who did.

But, these groups were very clearly defined.

It happened just like that, and for whatever reason, I was dismissed from my former friends who were now deemed 'popular.'

I won't ever forget how I felt about that, and as a consequence to being shunned from one social circle and forced into another, I developed a painfully shy complex.

I mean, even in junior high and high school it took everything for me to learn to look people in the eye, or feel good enough to be around people I just met. School was hard, because trusting others was difficult.

I didn't feel well liked, and for a long time, I felt like that was my reality. That's the way it was always going to be.

There are people who are well liked, and others who aren't—and I fell into the latter category.

What I NOW know after a few decades of experience being unpopular, years of research under my belt and becoming a likeability specialist is.

I have become someone that people gravitate towards.

In fact, it's funny, because once I entered my late 20's and I began to really go outside of my comfort zone and begin dating with confidence (something I had always been too shy and insecure to do before that), I receive the same compliment from every woman I entered into a relationship with.

The compliment was this: "There's just something about you," or "You just make me feel so good."

The 'something' that women felt when they dated me was drawing them into me, and they were drawn into me because I was someone who showed them those essential skills (you saw earlier...)

I showed them I was compassionate by listening to what they had been through, and not interrupting them while they talked to talk about myself.

I demonstrated confidence, by discussing experiences I've had in my life that I was proud of, because they all amounted to me becoming me. I even told a few people about my past shyness, and how I'm glad I used to be like that. When they asked why, I told them in a self- assured manner, because it makes me who I am today.

I demonstrated myself as a fun-loving person to be around, and with a positive state of mind.

Just think about it.

How many times have you talked to a significant other, a co-worker or a friend, and while the conversation starts off positive, it dips down to something negative? (People do this a LOT.)

Maybe they begin nagging at you, or complaining about the person they're telling the story about.

It immediately weighs you down, shuts you off emotionally and quickly, you can become disengaged in the other person.

I learned the importance of positivity when I got my first major career break.

Right after my new boss offered me the job (which I enthusiastically accepted), I said, "May I ask what made you choose me? (Especially since they were other candidates who were more highly qualified than I was).

He looked at me and said assertively, "Because you can write and you're positive." That was it.

Positivity (among other traits) draw people in, giving you the ability to have auto-magnetism work at your disposal—any time and all the time.

Everyone wants to be liked, but most people don't know what it really takes, so they continue to do what they've always done.

They remain in their comfort zone.

Or, perhaps they adapt a shyness condition (like I used to) or become highly defensive about others in order to protect themselves from getting hurt, or rejected.

The fact is, likeability is a learned trait, but it's also your right.

You have a right to be well liked, to be admired, and to be acknowledged for the unique traits you offer others. You're unique—no one can do what you do in the very same way that you can do it.

(The key is remembering that, so you can project a whole new type of energy, which will allow you to shift what and who you bring into your life.)

This is exactly why I've written this book – to provide the kind of instant, intimate feedback that millions look for and don't know where to get it.

This book is your blueprint to becoming well liked for a lifetime.

Dating

"There are only two ways to live your life. One is as though nothing is a miracle. The other is as though everything is a miracle."

– Albert Einstein

As I mentioned before, men and women naturally seek out partners with positive energy.

Life long bonds are formed between men and women who know how to mutually make each other's lives better.

People who are more generally likeable tend to have more success when it comes to relationships and marriage.

So developing likeability traits is not only important for your romantic relationships but also for your friendships and work life relationships...

Create a powerful, likable personality and you'll have prospective partners coming after you, your personality attracting them like flies to honey.

Friendship

"Friendship is always a sweet responsibility, never an opportunity.

– Khalil Gibran

Got friends?

If you don't, then you're probably feeling like there's a gap in your life, and that's because no matter how amazing your romantic relationship is or how thriving your career/business may be, friendship is what holds it all together.

While you're in school, it's easy to have an instant group of friends, but if you're like me (upon entering the workforce and going in a whole new direction as you social circle from school went), life can get lonely especially when you expect a whole new flock of friends to follow you there.

I remember when I took a marketing job at a non-profit in my mid-20's. It was my first 'real job'.

I had a small cubicle.

I had an hour for lunch.

I had a line-up of meetings to go to every day of the workweek.

But, I also lost my social circle of people to bond with, talk to and commiserate over.

My buddies from college had become lawyers, or international travellers, and in my new life, I didn't know how or where I was going to meet people.

At this time, I still had some shy tendencies from my youth, and being in a new work environment (after years of having a blast in my comfort zone during college) made me feel vulnerable all over again.

So, here's what I did...

I took just one step outside of my comfort zone, to build up a habit of talking to others (in order to feel more comfortable and well liked in social settings.)

The fact is (and I've learned this the hard way), sticking to yourself, being unwilling to take risks, focusing on the negative and refusing to connect with others is a recipe for disaster.

Not only does it keep you stuck emotionally, but it does the opposite of magnetizing yourself to others – because people don't want to be around someone who has those traits.

It doesn't offer anyone anything good. People are drawn to positive, energetic, fun loving and compassionate people. So, I developed a little game for myself.

Since I was working the hardest I've ever worked in my life and didn't know where I could meet likeminded people (in order to create a new social circle for myself), I developed the 'coffee shop charisma' game.

It works like this...

The Coffee Shop Charisma Exercise

Find a place you go to frequently.

In my case, it was the neighbourhood coffee house right next to my apartment building. When I began this exercise, all of the baristas already knew my face, but they didn't know my drink.

They didn't know my name because I never introduced myself by saying a friendly, "Hi, I'm Mark!"

So, every morning, I walked into that neighbourhood coffee house and started to smile while making eye contact with the people there.

I'd smile at the barista who took my order, and made eye contact with the woman who made my drink.

I'd smile while walking past the other customers.

Then, as the days went on, I began talking to strangers I would meet there. I'd say anything from "I come here way too often, what about you?" to "Gorgeous day, isn't it?"

If I saw a beautiful stranger in line, I'd approach her and say hi.

Or I might just smile and see if she worked up the nerve to talk to me. If she didn't, I'd say something like, "I think you're in here as much as I am!" (which would always result in a conversation, and sometimes, a phone number.)

Pretty soon, and before I got to the front of the line, those amazing baristas would have my drink ready to go for me.

They began talking to me, and after about a month, I knew all of their names, and they knew mine.

They knew about my job and my addiction to camping (and pretty much anything outdoors.)

I knew about their kids, and their spouses, and the demand of their school and work schedules. We sympathized over this crazy thing called life. We even had conversations about love.

It began to feel like a little family in there.

Then something interesting happened. I don't know if it's because I started smiling at them, or chatting with them as I put the cream and sugar in my coffee, but they began giving me my daily, morning drink for free.

They refused to let me pay for it. Something had shifted, and it was permeant.

I didn't realize what was happening while I was doing it, but I had become so likeable, that they were extending themselves to me (which they didn't do for any other customer.)

This was one of many experiences I've had in my life which I've seen auto-magnetism at work, without me having to manipulate anyone, or 'try too hard' to get others to like me to make friends and to create opportunities in my life without struggling to obtain them.

I remember one time I brought my mom in there for a cup of coffee. She wanted to treat me to a latte, and I said, "You can try to give them money, but I don't think they'll take it."

She looked at me, confused. I said, "Just watch this. It's unbelievable." We ordered a medium latte and a large mocha.

My mom handed them her credit card, and they looked at me, and smiled. I asked the barista how her baking class is going, and she enthusiastically replied, "It's awesome. I'm learning so much!"

Then she said, "This must be your mom!" and shook my mom's hand. She then told my mom to put her credit card away, that it wasn't any good here.

Our drinks were waiting for us on the bar, and after taking a few sips, my mom said, "How do you do that?"

I replied, "I'm not really doing anything. I'm just interested in their lives I guess."

The fact is, I am genuinely interested in their lives, in people's lives in general—and that's what friendship is really about. Showing care, interest and compassion in what the other person is going through.

It's about being positive and cheerful with a 'glass is half-full' attitude to life. It's about extending yourself for another, and making other people's lives better.

It's about having the confidence to be yourself around others, and making other people feel great about themselves when they're around you.

(Further in this book, you'll learn how to do all of these by cutting away any unfriendly behaviours you have lingering in your social playbook, learning how to talk to someone in any situation, become funny and interesting, and generate other people's interest, day by day.)

Work

How many times have you reintroduced yourself to your boss or someone else upstairs? How many times have you tried to get their attention and froze up? Perhaps you don't get the respect that you deserve in the workplace? The workplace is one of the hardest places in life to stand out and get ahead.

People are busy and don't have time to stop and talk to every co-worker or subordinate with an agenda.

But the likable people?

The funny, interesting, engaging people who everyone wants to have lunch with? They create a gravitational field in which bosses, co-workers and clients will come to them. And you can too.

Impressing Your Family

We rarely think about the effects of a likable personality on our families, but consider this.

How much easier would holiday dinners with your in-laws be or conversations with your parents if you were more likable, engaging and funnier in conversation?

Yeah, they love you, but with the tips in this guide, you'll soon find that they will like you too.

Likeability is a Learned Trait (and I'm Here to Teach It To You!)

Relationships are tricky things. Even if you've been married for twenty years, what do you think will happen as you age and you grow even more introverted?

Your spouse will grow bored and while love can persist, the excitement of marriage can grow stale. The same can be true for your friendships and family connections – all of which can grow brittle and drift apart.

The tips in this guide are going to reinvigorate how you talk to people you know and love and create a new personality that they will absolutely love to be around.

But, it takes some work on your part. There isn't a switch in the back of the human brain you can just flip and instantly become that person at every party you attend.

There's a Science to Likability

Psychologists, anthropologists and biologists have been studying the interactions of human beings for as long as we've been able to observe, write, and discuss all the silly things we do.

It's become an area of special interest to me in recent years because it represents so many theories and possible solutions for how we actually become likable.

Don't worry; I'm not going to get too carried away unloading theories behind social psychology on you.

But I do want to share with you some of the more interesting ideas that have been posited in the last hundred years or so about why we do the things we do and what people actually expect from one another.

For example, how often to you make judgments about your own abilities based solely on what someone else can do?

Children with overachieving older siblings do this all the time – feeling like failures because they don't live up to big-bro or big-sis in every possible category. It's called social comparison theory and it has been around since the 1950s.

Another popular theory that I've studied a lot is Observational Learning.

It states that our behaviour is acquired through observation, by following the lead of others instead of through reinforcement or negative reinforcement.

It's how our children learn to walk and talk and it's how I'm going to show you to be more sociable and cut out those unfriendly tendencies you've developed that hinder social interactions.

In some situations, you might even come across social exchange theory – the idea that people will only put as much into a relationship as they feel they will benefit. It's a business- like way of approaching love and friendship and while it may sound silly, it's all around you.

How many times have you thought to yourself "what's in it for me" when someone asks you for a favour?

How often have you been given the third degree about your intentions when you ask someone else for a favour?

Not everyone does this, and honestly I wish no one did, but it's a very real part of most relationships and something you need to take into account if you're going to be successful – especially when you first meet someone.

In order to develop auto-magnetism, you need to come from a place of giving, not taking.

Wouldn't it be amazing to get what you want, without ever having to ask, beg or merely hope you'll get it?

It's called the giving box...

...and I've first headedly seen it work for my best friend and her husband who began implementing this technique in their love life when they were facing communication issues, and problems coming together and agreeing on everything in their marriage.

Now happily married, they credit the giving box to what changed it all around, allowing them to approach their relationship from a generous state (which has shifted their entire relationship around.)

Now, before I go into the giving box exercise, it's important that you understand not just how it works...

But why it can work on anyone, no matter what age they may be, or what state of the relationship they may be in with you.

There are research based, universal truths that make relationships work, simply because despite the differences between man or woman, deep down, we want the same things.

In order to cultivate a deeper love, appreciation and romance from your partner, you need to tap into your partner's core needs and deepest desires. When you do, he/she will willingly give you everything you could ever want.

- Your partner needs respect. Respecting the one you're with is about valuing what they offer in the relationship, and who they are as an individual.

Trying to change their behaviour communicates disrespect, while asking for their opinion, placing value in their advice; work ethic or perspective is respectful.

Respecting your partner isn't just about stroking his ego or making her feel like a queen.

When you show that you accept your partner for who they are and what tremendous gifts they bring to your happiness, it can significantly increase the passion, and your emotional connection to one another.

Some of the happiest couples can be seen working together, such as building a garden in their backyard, or exercising at the gym together. Respect is about building one another up, and working together to come up with a solution for the greater good of the relationship—and each person in it.

- Show appreciation. Everyone needs to be appreciated, and the longer you're in a relationship, the more essential that becomes.

What motivation will your partner have to be caring, kind and considerate with you when he doesn't even think you value him enough to do the same for him?

Anytime your partner feels appreciated by you, he/she feels love.

That's how love is often communicated—by demonstrating that you value what he/she does for you and your happiness.

Attraction really is about honoring the small contributions that your partner makes on a day-to-day basis.

If your partner fills up your gas tank without ever mentioning it, show thanks. If your partner rubs your feet while you watch a movie on the couch, show her with a kiss or loving embrace that you're thankful for her.

So, in order to give your partner a sense of admiration and appreciation, you need to know the right way to give it (learn all about their love language in chapter 13!)

While women and men have similar, deeply rooted and primal needs, they receive them in different ways. Here's a breakdown of what women and men need in order to feel appreciation clearly:

- Women—need to feel reassured that her partner is faithful, devoted to her (and only her), respected, cared for, protected and understood.
- Men – need to feel first and foremost respected by his partner, trusted, admired, approved and encouraged.

There are many ways to demonstrate this, which will be covered in detail in chapter 11.

You don't have to change who you are or what you need in a relationship to make your partner happy. You simply need to know how they clearly feel respected, loved and admired by you—in order to cultivate a greater love with each day that passes.

- Become solution oriented as a couple. This is one of the mistakes that intimacy experts see happen again and again in relationships, and what accounts for thousands of divorces each year.

The common pitfall in relationships—when a couple experiences a hiccup, miscommunication or are at odds about something—is to act at war with one another, and fixate on the problem.

The problem really isn't the problem, itself.

It's the length of time that they focus on the problem. The longer they talk, dwell or hash out the details of 'who did what', the greater risk for blame negativity, anger, frustration, and criticism to take place.

When you become solution oriented—that is, you're focused on working on the solution instead of being focused on the problem— you can quickly reinstate your desire for the person you're with, and communicate respect and love instead.

The Giving Box

The giving box mentality is all about exactly what you may have guessed—a focus on giving to others instead of taking.

A while back I saw a three minute video from one of my personal mentors, Tony Robbins.

In this video, he talked about what really brings on a successful relationship of any kind— romantic, friendship, parent to child, child to parent or professional.

It's a giving state.

It's focusing on what you're giving to that person (which instantly brings you happiness as well as bringing the other person happiness) and allows the relationship to prosper.

However, most people don't do this. They focus on what they're getting instead.

Take my good friend Sarah and her husband Tom. They've been married for over ten years now, and during that time, they've had some major ups and downs.

When things aren't great—Sarah is complaining about how she is always stuck doing the dishes after they entertain their friends, and Tom is always feeling blamed for her unhappiness (but at the same time, refuses to help her do the dishes)—they stay in their bickering mode for days even weeks, sometimes.

This is because their state of mind never changes.

They are both keeping a mental 'tally' of who did what, and how long it's been since they felt appreciated or loved.

But, if you come from a place of giving, appreciation and generosity, your entire relationship can shift.

That boss who doesn't even credit you or promote you may see your giving spirit as 'manager material,'

...Or your boyfriend/husband or girlfriend/wife who seems to nag you, might see your thoughtfulness as the very reminder she needs to focus on her appreciation for you...

When you come from a giving state.

All you need to do in order to implement the giving box into your life, is begin being aware of every relationship you have as a box, or a bank.

It doesn't exist without you, and the other person.

You can only fill the box each time you contribute something positive to the relationship: a thoughtful gesture, a compliment, sensitivity, compassion, a random act of kindness or being actively engaged in a helpful way.

This goes for the other person in the relationship as well.

You want to fill this giving box up, every single day...because every single day the box starts off empty again.

The more you fill it up with love, gratitude and thoughtfulness for the other person, the more they'll be likely to reciprocate and fill your life up with those same things.

While every relationship in your life is different from the next, one thing is constant, and it's something I've learned time and time again in my own relationships.

Everyone wants to feel special. Everyone wants to be heard and understood.

When you come from a giving state, you won't just have the power to improve your relationships (making them radically happier and more meaningful than you could ever hope for)

You'll have the power to transform how people react and respond to you.

No one theory can capture the mindsets of every individual you run into. But whenever you feel the urge to get down on yourself or to think there's something wrong with your worldview, remember that there are other people out there who not only think the same as you, but likely have the exact same problems.

In a world with such a vast, diverse population, you're never alone in how you think and those other people have likely found ways to be more successful in their relationships. And so can you.

Chapter One:

Why We Want to Be Liked

"No matter what he does, every person on earth plays a central role in the history of the world. And normally he doesn't know it." — Paulo Coelho, The Alchemist Ask anyone on the street whether they want to be liked and you'll get an emphatic "Yes."

The truth is that few of us can think of a tangible reason we want to be liked, but in reality, there are dozens of reasons - socially, professionally, and romantically - that drive us to seek the interest of our fellow humans.

- We want to feel validated;
- We want to be admired;
- We want to feel special;
- We want a connection with others who understand what we're going through;
- We're social, and want a network of others to spend time with;
- We want opportunity;
- We want love;
- We want fame;
- We want to be happy;

We want to experience life as much as possible, and become energized by others to   better ourselves (as much as possible).

We like to be liked - simple as that. Being likable isn't just about getting something out of other people (though it can have a huge impact on how likely a friend or family member is to help you out). Being likable also actually results in behaviours that lessen the likelihood of heart disease, stress related illnesses and general displeasure.

The stuff you're about to learn will not only help you make new friends and do better at work, it will help you feel better. You'll literally improve your body's ability to fight disease and stay balanced on a daily basis. Pretty cool, huh? And it's not just science that has made likability such a powerful goal to attain.

Historically, being likable has been the key to success in almost every area of life. Take for example Gallup Presidential polls in the United States.

Since 1960, likability has been the only single factor that every winning candidate has taken an edge in. You want to be president? You'd better be more likable than your opponent.

We want likable people to be in charge and we want likable people to win – that's why we always root for the underdog.

Even without knowing a single thing about a team, they are immediately likable in our minds because they take on the role of the perpetual David to whichever Goliath happens to be their opponent.

In the Goliath Syndrome, the idea is that most of us feel meek and underappreciated, or generally trod upon by bigger and better people.

So, when someone is successful as an underdog – as the downtrodden little guy – we feel an immediate connection to them. In this, likability is an extension of our self-image. We like that which we aspire to be and which we can relate to.

And other people will like that which they aspire to be as well. If you can become that ideal friend, partner, family member or co-worker, you will always be the most likable man or woman in the room.

Likeability is being part of the team—someone who everyone loves and admires, but it's also about setting yourself apart as someone who has something amazingly valuable to offer.

It could be your crazy sense of humor, or your ability to talk to anyone about anything (in any setting.)

It could be your ability to make red velvet cupcakes, or your thoughtful habit of making gifts for everyone at the office, several times a year, "just because."

(Talk about a likeable trait!)

In order to really begin using the techniques and exercises you'll find in this book, my clients have found this one exercise in particular to be a great beginner exercise to start doing.

It will shift your perspective from a doubtful one to a winning one...

...and showcase just what you have to offer to others—which will make you a likeable person with any crowd, right off the bat.

I think of it as a visual reminder that promotes confidence and charisma. Here's how to do it:

- Take out a piece of paper, and a pen, and set aside about twenty minutes, free of distraction.
- Set the timer (only twenty minutes, so you don't start crossing things off or thinking too hard.)
- Write down as many things as you can about your personality that you love, are proud of, or simply make you, 'you'.
- Examples could be: "my love for taking pictures," or "my past experiences with traveling the world," etc.
- Make sure to include experiences you've had that set you apart (could be personal or professional..)
- Include lessons you've learned, perspectives on different areas of your life (what have you learned about people, love, the opposite sex, yourself?)
- Over the next week or two, feel free to add to this list.
- Tape it up on your bedroom wall, refrigerator door or bathroom mirror and look at it every day.
- Remind yourself of how great you are, how awesome you've become, how smart and wise life experience has made you.
- Re-read your list twice a day: once when you are getting ready for work in the   morning, and once right before bed.

This list won't just remind you that you're the kind of person who deserves to be well liked. It will become internalized in you, so that whatever limiting fears you may have about yourself, can virtually become eradicated (in order to give you the ability to attract better experiences to you!)   Did you know that your body responds based on your social interactions?   Human beings are social animals.   We are born and hard wired to live in groups of between 50 and 100 people. Our memories are actually formed based on the number of people that tend to exist in an average person's social life. Why do you think you feel so much more creative at a coffee shop surrounded by perfect strangers, even with headphones in your ears? Or more energized after going on a date with someone you particularly like? It all comes down to neurological impact of social interaction - the release of dopamine that occurs when another human being gives you positive feedback, whether it is a laugh at your joke, a slap on the back or a request to spend more time together. Your body quite literally feeds on it and likeability makes it much more likely to occur. You want to be liked and your body will do what it can to make it happen.

Why Likability Impacts Your Life So Much

Your job, as you read this book is to start thinking about how people see you along with the choices they make about you.

By understanding what those choices are and how they are made, you can develop a sixth sense about what does and does not work in presenting yourself to others. The idea being that, when you fully understand the way your presence affects others, you'll be able to tweak your actions to get the result you want.

That may sound manipulative, but it doesn't have to be. Like any tool, it's all in how you use it. If you choose to go down the road of manipulation, yeah, likability can be a pretty powerful tool. But a big part of likability is having that power and not using it.

I could go on forever about the benefits of being likable – but you already have a goal in mind. You wouldn't be reading this if you didn't.

So, what I want to do now is tell you about a little secret – one of the most profound secrets that likable people everywhere hold over the quiet, dormouse guys and gals in society that just can't get any attention.

Likability isn't forced.

It's organic – which means three things. First, you have to feel the confidence inside that will make it happen.

Ever watch a woman walk into a bar and have men flock to her in droves? Or a man who can seemingly get a date with anyone?

Yeah, they're likable, but beneath that likability is something more – a sense of self that transcends simple surface traits. They are sure of themselves and we are all intoxicated by that powerful sense of self.

That's you – you have to be confident 100% of the time if you want to be even remotely successful in the dating world.

Here are some confidence tips I've used for years—and my philosophy has always been that if it can work on someone like me (someone who used to be so shy he couldn't even look at others in the eye), then it can work for you:

☐ ☐ Go outside of your comfort zone (just a little bit.) I know you may think, "If being confident was really that easy, I'd be the most confident person in the world by now," but the truth is, most of the time, we make it harder on ourselves than it has to be.

We actually spend about 50 percent of our day with unfocused thoughts—thoughts that wander from "what time is it" to "How can I make my presentation for that client more engaging," to "I wish I was eating a donut right now."

The truth is, you don't have to waste all of your energy on thoughts that don't matter. You can actually 'do' something instead of 'think' about it (and as a result catapult into a confident person within a very short time.)

The way to do this is by stepping outside of your comfort zone, just a little bit.

If you're used to doing the same types of activity during the weekend (and as a result, only run into the same people over and over again, making your feel like there isn't anyone to date, or new people to get to know), change your scene.

Try out a cardio class you've been wanting to take at a fitness studio you've been meaning to check out.

Take a painting or kayaking class to get to know other like-minded people, who share the same interests as you.

Or, if you want to meet someone special (and the dates you've been on have been a major bust), try online dating.

Create a profile that shows off your most confident, happy self. (For example, write about how you love trying new things, heading to music festivals or trying new restaurants, etc.)

- Smile, and give someone a compliment. Just think about it—when was the last time you received a compliment from someone?

Chances are, you probably can't remember. Most people don't come from a giving frame of mind, because MOST people are so consumed by their own lives that they are unable to step outside of themselves, and enjoy the person and/or the moment for what it is.

Gain confidence and credibility as a person (around all your encounter) when you stop, smile and give someone a compliment.

It could be something simple like, "I love that skirt. Where did you get it?"

Or, it could be something like, "I feel so much better after you showed me that little trick for my excel spreadsheet. Thanks!"

Compliments make people feel good, and when you genuinely give someone a compliment (make sure it's sincere, because people can pick up on inauthentic statements).

When you make people feel good, they'll associate you with feeling good...talk about a secret skill that will get you allow you to become more popular than you could have ever hoped for!

- Become a skilled daydreamer. I'm a big believer in using my mind to achieve what it is I want most in life.

Whether you want to have an active dating life, a thriving career, the ability to become thin and fit, or cultivate a happier and more harmonious romantic relationship with your partner, becoming a skilled daydreamer is your shortcut there.

Here's why: your subconscious mind is flooded with thoughts, emotions and attitudes, many of which you learned by observing others or experiencing early in life.

Unfortunately, some of these thoughts, emotions and attitudes are limiting and negative.

A thought may be, "I can't ever lose this weight, so why even try?" It's these subconscious thoughts that guide our actions, and which dictate our behaviours.

It can stop us from having more money, better opportunities, and a greater love.

But, the good news is, that you can actually change your subconscious thoughts by re-programming your conscious mind.

I do this by becoming a self-proclaimed 'daydreamer at the expert level.'

(My friend's used to laugh at this, until I began getting the career and financial opportunities they've only dreamed of getting!)

By focusing on an image in my mind (such as imagining myself playing basketball with a whole team of people who are my good friends and colleagues), I can convince myself that I, in fact, have this in my life...

...and improve my confidence.

The first key to doing this well is by coming up with one ideal image—something you want to have in your life—and imagine it over and over.

Daydream about it (with intention, as though it's actually happening in reality) several times a day. Do more if you can.

The second key to improving your confidence through daydreaming is visualizing it while BELIEVING it.

In other words, don't just go through the motions and think, "Aw, it sure would be nice to have someone amazing in my life."

Believe it is happening right now, as though you are the miracle worker in your own life who has a magic wand.

You're the holder of your dreams, and you can either manifest them or block from appearing in your life RIGHT NOW.

Daydream by focusing on the emotion.

So, if you want to have the confidence to make a crowd of people laugh, daydream about speaking to others, and hearing their laughter echo the room.

Watch their smiling faces, and feel yourself as a powerful, comedic presence in their life—and as someone they can depend on to feel better, based upon your ability to tell a great joke, or to be a skilled storyteller.

Repetition works. Capture the image of what you want in your mind, and practice dreaming with intention...

Knowing that whatever it is you want to accomplish, will come true.

It's just a daydream away. In order to become credible, it's important to stop worrying about what other people think.

More specifically, you must abandon the thoughts that have been plaguing you since the last outing you made.

Did someone laugh at your hobbies? Ignore you altogether? Forget your name? It doesn't matter.

When you meet someone for the first time, they will make a series of snap judgments about the kind of person you are and whether they are interested in talking to you.

If you sit there and worry about mistakes you've already made, they will be judging that same mistake prone person you were weeks or months ago.

Let it go – be someone interesting, new and exciting.

Only then can you build the rapport that will generate likability. We'll work on this a LOT in the coming chapters, so don't feel like it's something you should just know off the bat.

Finally, the third thing that natural likability needs is honest, truthful compassion and empathy for the person you're meeting.

Think of it this way...

...If someone walked up to you in a bar, was perfectly pleasant and listened to you carefully, but about an hour in decided to drop hints that they are really only interested in sex, what would your response be?

Whether you go home with them or not is irrelevant – you probably won't like them, though. And that's because there's no reason to.

They're being selfish and closed minded, and they probably weren't listening to much of what you had to say other than to close the deal.

You must care and pay attention, engage in their interests and be truthfully interested in their needs, wants and desires if you want the person you've just met to like you. This is a big area that a lot of people have trouble with.

The Game Changer of a Technique I've Used For Years...

I want to introduce something to you I call the Credibility Magnet technique. This technique is something I have personally used in my social life—even back to the days when I was painfully shy.

Back then, all I wanted to do was make friends but it was very difficult for me, with a lifetime of negative thoughts preventing me from even being able to make eye contact with others.

If you want to be well liked, you need to be in a position for people to take you seriously— plain and simple. In order to do that, you need to achieve the respect of others around you. People who are popular have something to stand on.

It might be a career that they are extremely knowledgeable in (and can teach others about). It might be your killer taste in clothes—no matter what it is, it's something that commands respect.

This technique is about commanding respect, so that you immediately build credibility in the eyes of others, set yourself apart from every other person out there, and as a result, instantly make others become magnetized to you.

Here's how to do it:

- Think of a passion of yours. This could be something that you love to do as a hobby, or it could even be your career.
- Make a list of everything you love about it. Let's say you love to stay active with different forms of exercise: CrossFit, yoga, hiking, rock climbing, and weight lifting/resistance training. Make a list of everything you love about that hobby of yours. It could be that you love how it makes you feel while doing it, or you love the payoff (a fit body that rocks!), improved body confidence, a great activity to do with friends, etc.
- Stare at that list every day, if only for a minute. Post it on your bathroom mirror, and soak it in. These are the things that will make you unique, which will increase your confidence, which will improve your credibility factor, which will get you WELL LIKED.

Now, you may read this and think, ok.... but how do I deal with those mean, rude, difficult- to-handle people that treat me like a doormat no matter WHAT I do?

I want to introduce a technique I designed after one friend of mine in particular had a son who was being bullied in school. This kid was a

34

good kid—smart, kind, caring, and a great friend to his buddies. In fact, he was a good friend to everyone. But, he was also very sensitive.

At ten years old, he was already beginning to internalize other people's opinions of himself, which led to the occasional tears (which unfortunately, happened in front of crowds of his peers on the playground.)

I'm not a fan of violence, so my advice wasn't to lash out, and stand up for himself by means of fighting. However, I do think it's important to have a strong backbone, and a strong backbone means you have BOUNDRIES that no one crosses, ever.

Apply the reverse doormat technique, and you'll be able to send out a nonverbal, highly effective message to people everywhere—you're not to be messed with, but respected; you're not a victim, but a survivor.

Now, this technique is so easy to do, it really doesn't matter what your age is or confidence level may be. My friend's son was able to use it despite the extreme stress he was under from his bully—and in my experience, if he can effectively pull this off, any adult can.

Let me first explain what happened prior to him using this technique, so that you have a reference for using it in your own life. 24 hours before he used this technique, he came to his mom and I about a bully named Steven.

Steven was bigger, louder and rough. Naturally, he found someone (my friend's son) who was physically smaller and emotionally softer than he to pick on. This guy went up to my friend' son and said, "Tomorrow in the playground after school. Let's see in front of everyone who's stronger when I beat you down."

This kid was in the sixth grade classroom, and known for picking on someone new every other week.

Unfortunately, my friend's son was this week's target. Telling his mom and I what happened, he was sobbing, petrified that the next day, he would get beaten up by the most feared kid in school.

This is what I told him to do: "This bully is desperate for some kindness in his life. But, he also needs to know that you aren't going to accept his tempting offer to fight him tomorrow.

So, I'm going to teach you how to walk and talk like you mean business – without ever having to come close to actually fighting him—because what I'll teach you will nip it in the bud so fast that he won't know what hit him."

I taught my friend's son how to walk with his shoulders back. I gave him a tip for reducing the nervousness, and I told him how to speak with confidence, using sales 'close the deal' statements so that bully would have NO CHOICE but to accept what he said. And, I taught him how to swap his 'offer' of a fight for another offer.

It worked. My friend's son walked right up to him the next day, as soon as the bell for recess began.

His shoulders were back, his smile was on, and before the bully could say or do anything intimidating, my friend's son said the following: "Hey, I heard you wanted to see that new Superman movie that came out. Thought you might want to go, I bought an extra ticket, so you could have it if you want it."

The bully looked right at my son's friend and couldn't speak. I had instructed him to 'close the deal' as quickly as he could, so he responded with, "I'll bring you the ticket tomorrow. It's for Saturday. I'll just meet you at the theatre at 12?"

"Y-y-y-eah," said the bully, who in just one moment's time had gone from intimidator to the one being intimated.

That bully never bothered him again. In fact, these two former enemies went through the rest of their primary education being nice, civil and best of all, respectful of each other.

Something so simple as this reverse doormat technique has the power to turn anyone into a commander of respect, confidence and likeability. It works especially well with difficult people, or simply people you may be intimidated by.

Here's how to do it:

- Look at yourself in the morning and tell yourself how amazing you are. This step is so important because it shifts how you feel about yourself—and what the mind believes, you can truly achieve. Don't want to be a doormat any longer? Then convince yourself you aren't—which is why you need to teach yourself through repetition that you aren't.
- Repeat the mantra: "Kill them with kindness." Repeat this mantra throughout your day, and remember the story I just told you about the bully. The proof is all right there.

Most people, who are difficult to work with, simply need love the most. You can completely transform your relationship with people by giving them the thing they really want—a good listener, an empathetic ear, or even a compliment.

- Close the deal. The most important step of the reverse doormat technique, especially when you're dealing with feelings of insecurity or fear. When my friend's son approached that bully, do you think he was scared? Of course he was. He was petrified. That's why you have to practice looking and walking the part.

But, the real key is closing the deal (just like salespeople do). Before the other person has a chance to turn you down or say no to what you're offering, lock up the conversation with a closing statement. Something like, "I'll see you at 10. Looking forward to it!" Be positive, sincere, and blow them away with kindness.

In any capacity of your life, you can become the person you really want to be. You can be popular. You can be surrounded by people who admire you, want the things that you want, and full of love and joy in their life. What makes you truly likeable is that you know how to work it. There are guys and gals out there who love the same things as the people they meet and simply fail to convey it. It has the same effect as ignoring someone you just met – we're going to fix that, so keep reading.

What People Think About Us

"What others think about me is none of my business."

– Wayne Dyer

So, with all that said, what do people really think about you? I'm going to say something that goes against every emotion you've felt since you were five years old – it doesn't matter. It really doesn't matter, and here's why. When you meet someone for the first time, one of three things will happen:

1. They will be interested in what you have to say and want to hear more.
2. They will be put off by your personality or mannerisms and stop paying attention.
3. They will be too busy or simply unsure of you, so will stick around to see what you're all about.

In short, they'll have a strong positive, strong negative, or neutral reaction to you.

Once upon a time, we would be fearful of that strong negative – so much so that we'd avoid contact altogether.

It's an actual phobia – that fear of instant rejection.

Scientists call it Social Phobia and if you let it grow, it can cripple your ability to meet new people, talk to the people you already know and generally put yourself out there to be part of the greater discourse. In short, it's not good.

But, what we're doing in this book goes beyond all that.

We're creating a situation in which you know for a fact that you are being genial and likable, but more importantly, you will have the confidence to say "who cares" if someone has that strong negative reaction to you.

Only people with low self-esteem get worked up when someone decides they don't like them.

This is who you are – the whole person that you are proud of and confident in. If you decide to change that person and be someone other than who you have always been, what's the point of being a unique individual?

When you're a whole, complete person with an interesting life and a likable personality, the last thing on your mind will be 'what does this perfect stranger think of me?'

(Practice my confident tips which you just read about, and you'll be able to confidently assert who you are, without apologies.)

But, we're not there yet and I understand your concern. These interactions might be more than just casual encounters at a grocery store.

They could have a direct impact on your social and work standing for months or years to come. That's why you're here and that's why my likability book is going to change how you view your social interactions for good.

Sexual Confidence

There's something innately attractive about a likable person. Forget everything you see on TV about the rude, mean people who seem to get all the men or women. I'm talking about something different.

I'm taking about sexiness... ...sex appeal...

And in my experience (as well as the clients I've coached to be powerful and popular), sex appeal is all about confidence.

You don't have to be manipulative to get what you want. You don't have to be mean.

You don't have to puff out your feathers or wear designer clothes to get the attention of the opposite sex.

You don't have to complain to your significant other to get more sex, affection or thoughtful gestures of appreciation – because let's face it, did that ever work anyways?

The truth about sex appeal is that no matter whether you're a man or a woman, it comes to a sensual and a sexual confidence.

This confidence is so magnetizing because it draws people in, and it draws people in because these people who possess it are in control of their reality.

They dictate what will happen to them at every step of a relationship.

Yes we all want a partner who is intelligent and sure of themselves, but everyone wants a partner who is nice to spend time with. They want someone with a good sense of humour who can carry a conversation, will ask for an opinion, and generally engage anyone they meet.

They are strong, sure of themselves, and clear in their intentions.

They have boundaries, and at the same time, are open minded enough to enjoy life—no matter what may come.

They take care of their emotional and physical needs, without depending on someone else to do it for them. And, because they don't depend on anyone else to make them happy, they radiate sex appeal to everyone.

Have you ever wished you had the real secret to everlasting attraction—attraction that doesn't just come and go, but stays put in your life...for life?

Here's your blueprint for immediately showing off your best, most attractive self to others, which will effortlessly and reliably bring you more love, passion and desire than you'll know what to do with!

- If you're female, work your femininity. Femininity is what you inherently possess. Being a woman is a great thing, and a very attractive thing because at you core, you are giving nurturing, and loving.

You're gentle and kind, and a care taker for your family.

Most attractive of all, is your ability to feel emotions on a deep level and nurture your relationships—something that many men just don't have an easy, or natural time doing.

Many women make the mistake of hiding these traits, for feeling weak or vulnerable while in relationships.

But, it's what is so attractive about women.

You can instantly become someone who effortlessly magnetizes herself to men simply by embracing who you are, and what you inherently offer.

Work you femininity by smiling, opening yourself up to men, showing them who you are, what experiences you've been through and what you've seen, touched and felt in your life.

Being feminine doesn't mean acting manipulative or angry in order to get what you want. You don't have to complain or nag the man in your life in order to get him to change his behaviour (that probably won't work anyways.)

Your giving, loving demeanour is what will create a true flow, and an abundant outcome for your relationship.

Focus on the things that you already possess as a woman—your deep ability to feel your emotions, your capacity to love while still feeling vulnerable, and your big, giving heart. That is what will continue facilitating the attraction and desire in your romantic relationships.

- If you're male, work your masculinity. Being a man means that you have something awesome at your disposal...something that will immediately allow you to have a magnetizing kind of sex appeal that women will be drawn to for a lifetime your masculinity.

As a man you are naturally a protector, a provider and a skilled and shift decision maker.

You have the ability to know what decision should be made in order to please a client, or to take care of your family.

You're strong, and powerful in your convictions, and you're honest and blunt in your communication. You're independently minded, intelligent and decisive.

When you use this to your utmost ability, you become looked at as a strong, capable, and confident partner women are instantly drawn to.

You're a knight in shining armour. So when you bring your natural traits to the forefront in your relationship or dating life, and assert yourself as someone who knows who he wants (and actively pursues her), this is auto-magnetism at work.

It's simply harnessing who you are at your core, in order to make the person in your life feel really, really good.

- Accept the other person. So much of the time, we doubt ourselves, or try too hard to get the person we want, or wonder how we'll keep the attraction going.

The truth is, it simply takes bringing our natural gifts and strengths to the forefront, while accepting theirs at the same time.

Some women make the mistake of nagging, complaining or stonewalling (giving them the silent treatment, etc.) the man in their life as a punishment for him not giving her what she really wanted.

Some men 'tune' women out with work, or sports watching on TV, instead of spending time in the relationship, in order to make it better.

The reality is, the more time you put in your relationship, the better it becomes.

The more giving, thoughtful and mindful you are in regards to the other person, the more giving, thoughtful and mindful they will be with you.

Show the person you're interest in, dating or in ia relationship with that you're mentally, emotionally and physically invested...

...and all that takes is letting them know you're thinking of them.

Send them a text that says, "I miss you, I'm thinking of you and I can't wait to see you."

It could be that you go to their favorite department store on your lunch break and buy him/her a shirt you know they'd love...

...or you purchase their favorite meal from that Indian restaurant down the street from your house.

When it comes to relationships—and cultivating an intensely passionate, and seriously satisfying partnership, all it takes is some care, attention and the nurturing of the small details.

The small stuff ends up being really, powerful stuff—acts of kindness and thoughtfulness that you have the power to change at ANY point.

If you're not already, get excited – because this isn't just about being likable; it's about presenting the perfect version of yourself in a way that will become irresistible to everyone you meet.

Chapter Two:

Being Likable by Not Being Unlikable

The Power Of Friendship

In a 2009 article in the Health and Wellness section of the New York times, Tara Parker-Pope cited a study in which: "Researchers studied 34 students at the University of Virginia, taking them to the base of a steep hill and fitting them with a weighted backpack. They were then asked to estimate the steepness of the hill. Some participants stood next to friends during the exercise, while others were alone. The students who stood with friends gave lower estimates of the steepness of the hill. And the longer the friends had known each other, the less steep the hill appeared."

Think for a moment about the last time you met someone you didn't like. What do you remember about them? Was it how quiet they were or how they didn't engage the conversation? I doubt it. More than likely, the last person you remember not liking was boorish, obnoxious and rude.

There are two types of people who are not liked by others – the people who don't make an impression and therefore are not proactively liked or disliked and the people who are so obnoxious or rude that they instantly push you away from them.

And to put things in perspective, you don't have to be that obnoxious to be unlikable – in polite company, it doesn't take much.

I was always a quiet guy – I didn't think I was obnoxious at all, nor did I think I had any annoying habits or poorly worded statements.

But as I started to develop the personality that has made me friends, I learned one very important thing; you cannot be likable until you learn how not to be unlikable.

44

Everything in this book focuses on helping you stand out, be confident and interesting.

But, none of that does you any good if you also happen to take jabs at people you barely know, make degrading comments, or generally assume the worst about someone you just met. Sometimes, these things are merely bad habits.

Other times, they are the result of lot of cynicism built up over years of poor social skills. Whatever the problem, sociability starts with friendliness, and that's a little harder for some of us than for others.

Dumping the Unfriendly Traits

"Try a little harder to be a little better."

— Gordon B. Hinckley

Step one on the road to likability is recognizing the traits that stand out as being unlikable.

What are you doing right now that could make someone else cringe or stop listening? I guarantee you, from personal experience, that you probably don't realize you're doing any of them.

And don't think just because you're some kind of social savant with the people who do like you that you don't have any bad habits. Just ask your friends or family. I can guarantee they'll gladly point out the things on this list that fit your personality and probably offer you a few dozen tips on how to fix the problem.

There are a lot of things you never want to do to someone you like and respect, especially if you want them to like you.

With the help of a 2007 Johns Hopkins University study which analysed rude and unfriendly workplace behaviours, here is a list of things you may not realize you're doing that should stop immediately:

- Taking Credit for Someone Else's Work – If someone does something or broaches a topic, give them credit for the idea. One of the easiest ways to end a conversation is saying "Oh yeah, I heard that the other day and I also heard....." then going on as if you brought up the topic. It's a bad habit many people have as they try to be engaging in conversation but it generally alienates other people from speaking.

- Discrimination or Stereotyping – Simple enough; don't say anything rude about someone else's race, gender, age, sexual orientation, or any other differences. It's rude, closed minded and will almost always offend someone nearby. Discrimination goes even further – if you make a decision about someone based on anything but the key elements, you may be discriminating. This is a big one to look out for in dating.

- Talking Down to Other People – Talking down to someone in a position you deem "lower" than yourself is a sure way to alienate everyone you meet. Just because someone is bagging your groceries does not mean they are less intelligent or interesting than you. That could be your future spouse or a good friend, but instead of cultivating that relationship, talking down will create an uncomfortable situation every time you see them or their co-workers again.

- Inappropriate Jokes or Mocking – Making jokes or mocking someone is unfriendly in any situation. The only exception is if you already know someone, have established that kind of relationship and know that they will not be offended. Even then, make sure to gauge the limits of your joking, because it's very easy to go too far and create an uncomfortable situation.

- Littering and General Messiness – Just like your clothing and hair make statements about your self-esteem and confidence level, your general cleanliness in your office, car, or home will say a lot about the kind of person you are. If you're out with someone, find a garbage can for your empty coffee cup, not the bottom of a ditch.

- Technology Use During a Conversation – Nothing is less friendly than taking out a cell phone or checking your watch during the middle of a conversation. There is an unspoken subtext to these interactions that says "this is more important than our conversation". It will universally upset anyone you are spending time with and will make you seem like you don't care about their input.

- Patronizing – This is something that happens to a lot to parents, especially those who are impatient. Just because your five year old child needs a bit of help understanding a new concept does not mean your co-workers or a person you met in the bar need to be talked to like that. Nine times out of ten it's unintentional but the effect is just as unfriendly.

- Eye Rolling and Sarcasm – Imagine if someone you just met rolled their eyes at a statement you made or started making sarcastic statements about you or your conversation. How long would you stick around and continue talking to them? A lot of the time, people try to be playful or charming with sarcasm. It rarely works, so stick to easy things like non-personal jokes.

- Complaining and Whining – It may not seem unfriendly, but complaining or whining about something, even if it's unrelated to the person you're talking to will give the wrong impression. Complaints and general whininess make other people either uncomfortable or upset. On the flip side, if you maintain a positive tone in every conversation, they will feed on your positivity and want to be around you more often.

- Yelling or Unnecessarily Angry Outbursts – General anger is a turnoff to most people. It shows a lack of self-control, a short fuse, and a tendency to judge other people and events without all the facts. If you have a habit of growing angry at random events, take a step back and relax before engaging in conversation. Stick to positive actions and activities. Friendliness isn't hard. It's probably the easiest thing you'll learn in this book.

However, getting out and talking to strangers can be challenging at the beginning. That's why I put together some really easy ice-breakers, and exercises to help you do just that:

Kill them with kindness, every time. Whether you'd like to be more neighbourly with your neighbour, or you want to be able to achieve a greater comradery at work, kindness (genuine kindness) is the best way I've found to end fueds, and get people to come together with a common goal. Giving a compliment is one way to bring others together. Offering to solve a problem is another great way to bridge the gap between you and others.

Make small talk like a pro. If you find yourself at a work related dinner party (or a social one, in which you know the hostess, but that's about it), you can easily make small talk with others around you.

If you feel nervous, that's ok. Pick anything to talk about. It could be the huge menu that you feel overwhelmed by ("Have you ever seen so many salad options before? I haven't.") You can talk about anything related to the meal you're enjoying, or the restaurant you're dining at.

"I've never had Cuban food before, have you? I've always dreamt of going there. Have you travelled much?"

Going out of your comfort zone to play a sport or join a club or meet someone in a bar – those are hard. Being friendly to someone you just met? That's as easy as it gets. It just takes a different world perspective.

What's Got You Riled Up?

Nine times out of ten, the rudeness we show to others is misplaced. No, you shouldn't be a pushover, but why yell at the woman in Starbucks after a 5 minute wait in line? It's not her fault and she certainly cannot do anything about it.

You could just as easily have made a friend by telling a joke or making her feel better about what is most likely a stressful day, but instead you got rude and only made it worse.

Anger is one of those things that can severely interrupt even a good conversation. Have you ever had a friend or someone you're dating get angry in the car while driving? It's uncomfortable.

They yell, bang on the steering wheel, swear and do all sorts of things that you'd never do in front of someone from whom you want to gain respect. Even when you love that person, it's uncomfortable and slightly embarrassing.

Now, imagine doing that in front of a stranger and how do you think they would react?

I like to use the canine test for angry outbursts. I had a dog when I was younger who would grow anxious and leave the room if I got angry.

I could be yelling at my computer screen to vent at a crashed email client or grumble to myself about the weather or an annoying co-worker.

It didn't matter – if I grew actively angry, he would leave the room and get visibly upset.

Dogs are extremely empathetic creatures. They read body language, voice tone and facial expressions.

When the sum of the parts equals anger, they grow uncomfortable, even if it is not directed at them.

Guess what?

People do the same thing, just subconsciously.

Somewhere, hidden deep beneath our modern affectations and advanced language capabilities are vital, prehistoric reactions to body language and voice tone.

It's all still there.

Take a closer look the next time you're at the zoo to the interactions of chimpanzees or birds.

They preen, bounce, hop and move around to establish dominance, showcase strength and develop a pecking order that is ultimately going to determine who wins out in the fight for food and sex.

Whatever your beliefs, you should know that we do the same thing on a regular basis. The problem is that we don't always realize it and those messages get misinterpreted or directed at inanimate objects in ways that upset friends and strangers alike.

When I feel myself growing upset, I ask myself whether my actions would have upset my dog. If so, is it worth upsetting the dog?

It sounds like a strange test, but it really works.

The TV refusing to tune into a sitcom you want to watch is not worth upsetting your dog. Your boyfriend breaking up with you on the other hand is a very good reason to be angry and your dog is free to be equally as upset about it.

Don't take any of this as instruction to ignore your anger and cover it up. There's a reason we grow angry. It is a healthy release of stress energy.

It helps us deal with uncomfortable situations and to work through unhappy emotions. However, directing that anger at the wrong person or the wrong situation does you no good, and it can also be extremely damaging to your health.

Reducing Unfriendliness

"The only way that we can live, is if we grow. The only way that we can grow is if we change. The only way that we can change is if we learn. The only way we can learn is if we are exposed. And the only way that we can become exposed is if we throw ourselves out into the open. Do it. Throw yourself."

— C. JoyBell C.

Let's say you're a relatively nice person, you don't get overly angry at anything in particular and when someone gets to you know you, you're capable of a decent conversation for at least a few minutes.

Why then do you still come off as unfriendly?

No, you're not broken. It's not a personality disorder and you don't need pills.

More realistically, you're not even trying to be unfriendly – it's a combination of insecurity and discomfort in the presence of others that is causing your unfriendliness and nine times out of ten, simply recognizing that discomfort will help to reduce it.

I like to apply my three 'don't do' communication pitfalls.

It allows me to mend the 'disconnect' in my relationship, repair any miscommunication that has recently taken place, and communicate feelings of respect, admiration and appreciation for my partner.

No matter what type of relationship you're dealing with—a romantic one, a professional one or a personal one (such as with a family member, a neighbour, a parent at your kid's preschool, etc.) avoiding these following pitfalls can drastically heighten your popularity, improve your ability to get along with EVERYONE and reduce social blunders that can affect your social life.

- Being defensive. One of the fastest things you can do to emotionally distance your partner from you is by putting him/her on the defense.

Saying things to your partner like, "Why would I want to make you feel like that? I didn't do it on purpose!" or "Why haven't you asked me how I'm feeling when you know I've had a hard day today?" makes your partner feel like they are under attack.

Being in a relationship is about being on the same team, and sticking together when times are rocky. It's not about picking fights and playing on 'opposite teams or positioning yourself against the other.

Anytime you place blame on your partner, they feel backed into a corner, and as if nothing they say has an effect against what YOU'RE saying.

So, instead of using 'you" messages such as "You always take your friend's side against mine," or "You never tell me how beautiful I look anymore," use 'I' messages.

I messages are incredibly powerful, because they remove any opportunity for your partner to feel blamed, and instead create a statement of how you're feeling (which is hard for anyone to deny or fight against, as it's simply how YOU feel.)

"I felt hurt the other day when..." or "I know you didn't mean to come across this way, but I really miss when we used to plan date nights together. I cherish that time we have together, and would love to get back to that."

- Insulting your partner. Are you in a relationship in which you fight 'dirty'? If so, using a language full of insults is one of the fastest ways to turn your once healthy relationship into a destructive one (and possibly headed for a breakup).

Otherwise known as contempt, insulting your partner is any language or behaviour that is threatening, demeaning or 'below the belt' (such as comments that push their buttons.)

Insulting your partner puts you at war against him/her instead of working together to find the solution. The problem is, when you use contempt against the one you're in a relationship with, all 'rules' are out the window.

The name calling can begin.

The physical or emotional threats can ignite a whole new standard for fighting—now and for the future of your relationship. The sense of respect, admiration and appreciation your partner felt is now gone.

Perhaps worse of all, it sets a new standard for your relationship—that at any time, you can declare war on your partner, and for any reason because contempt is an emotional, irrational state to be in.

Contempt can be anything degrading, such as comments like, "You're a moron. Why would you think I would want you to do that?" or eye rolling after your partner says a grammatically incorrect sentence.

The undertone of that is a clear message of, "You're stupid, and I'm smart," or "You're right and I'm wrong."

You can change how you talk, communicate and address your feelings in a relationship before they have a negative impact.

Even when you're in disagreement, you can contribute something positive, and help mend the 'disconnect' without name calling, threats or negative body language.

Learn to be aware of your micro body expression that tell your partner what you're really thinking, before you even say a thing.

It could be learning to monitor an eye roll, or a frown that you make every time you see your partner doing something you don't approve of.

Or, it could mean taking a deep breath before you speak, so that you give yourself a second to sensor what you want to say in order to assess what you should say.

- Stonewalling. If you haven't heard of the term, stonewalling, before, there's a good chance you've participated in it a time or two.

Stonewalling is when one person is upset, communicating or trying to explain their viewpoint on something, and you dismiss them by ignoring them, or 'shut them out.'

If you're doing the stonewalling, it could because you're so frustrated, that the only behaviour you think might get the attention you want is by ignoring that they are even in the room.

But, for the person being stonewalled, it feels like they are being ignored, and that their position in the relationship is being invalidated.

Have you ever given someone the silent treatment before?

Yep—we are all guilty of it a time or two. Unfortunately, stonewalling someone doesn't solve a thing, and it can cause the other person to become more defensive.

A better solution is to practice active listening, which is listening without emotionally reacting.

Allow the other person to say whatever it is they need to say (showing that you're listening by nodding or saying, "I understand" is a good idea) and then responding by repeating back what you think they just said.

You can also practice breaking the stonewalling pattern altogether by helping the person who is doing the stonewalling to come to a less emotional state.

Ask them questions, using positive statements to calm down by saying things like, "I know you're upset and I want to help us come to a solution as quickly as I can, so that we are both happy again.

Can you tell me what's bothering you? I'd really like to know."

- Nagging. Nagging is one of the most unproductive relationship behaviors you can fall into. I don't believe it's something that anyone wants to do.

You don't wake up and say, "Geez, I'm really sick and tired of my husband coming home late from work, until well after the dinner has gotten cold.

So, my new approach is nagging at him about it until he does what I want him to do." No one thinks like that.

Unfortunately, nagging is a result of frustration, anger or simply feeling like you've exhausted everything else you can think of doing...so instead of asking for what you want (assuming that won't work), you whine, complain, criticize or nag.

The problem is, in my experience and virtually all of my friend's experiences in their romantic relationships, nagging creates a defensive reaction in the person being nagged at.

And, for the person doing the nagging, it creates even more frustration than he/she began with!

Instead of nagging, criticising or complaining about what you're not getting (romantic flowers sent to your workplace, sweet words of appreciation, more frequent date nights, more frequent sex, etc.) represent the change you WANT to see in your relationship.

For example, if you want more romance from your partner, be romantic towards them first. Send them flowers. Or, cook them a romantic meal.

Stop the nagging, and replace it with passionate kissing.

Or, simply tell the man/woman in your life how much they mean to you—and leave it at that.

A simple gesture holds the potential for really great things—things that can shift the entire dynamic of your relationship.

Set the tone for what you want, and they'll likely reciprocate it!

Not Everyone Is Out to Get You

Pretty simple advice here – stop assuming the worst about everyone you meet. I know you've done it – I've done it and I'm pretty good at being introspective of my reactions to other people. It's a bad habit that insecurity brings on and constant social interaction can make worse.

For example, when I go to the Post Office, I work hard to avoid the assumption that whoever helps me will be angry, tired, and impatient. Sure, sometimes they are all of those things, but other times, they are just a little tired.

If you treat them rudely because you assume they'll do the same to you, guess what? They will be rude.

However, if you treat everyone you meet with kindness – smiling, speaking nicely, and wishing them a good day, even the most annoyed workers are likely to at least grace you with a smile.

You won't solve this problem overnight. It's something that happens without us even realizing it most of the time. It's a coping mechanism that helps us prepare for what we think will be uncomfortable situations.

Build a Friendly Mind-set

What causes us to be rude to someone we've never met before? F. Scott Fitzgerald, the American author of The Great Gatsby once said "It's not a slam at you when people are rude – it's a slam at the people they've met before."

While Fitzgerald's tongue was firmly in cheek, there is plenty of truth to his statement. Unfortunately, most people won't think to themselves "oh, they're just upset at someone else." They'll see your anger and wonder why you could possibly be upset at theme based on the very limited interaction you've had.

It happens because you're not in a friendly frame of mind to start with. Mind-sets have been scientifically proven to have a significant impact on the nature of our social interactions. A mind set is more than just a way of looking at the world – it's the current framework you take into any conversation.

It's how you see things. If a certain kind of politics or religion makes you angry, you're far more likely to mistreat someone that defines themselves in those ways, even if they are incredibly interesting and likable.

With that in mind, it's no wonder that people are so quick to go after people they don't know, making snap judgments, getting angry over small slights and generating enmity with people they might never see again (or worse, people they will see every day). There are stressed out, angry at people who will always be generally unhappy in the world. But, it doesn't have to be like that.

A few simple adjustments to your mind set can make it far easier to be nice to the random strangers you run into each day.

Ideally, your goal should be to always go into a situation with a positive thought in mind. If someone runs into you at the grocery store, don't immediately think "that person isn't paying attention and is rude", think "maybe they are distracted by their own concerns and could use a smile right now to cheer them up."

You could be wrong.

They could be a complete jerk, but what if they were? Do you really think someone so callous they just run into people without a thought would be affected by your rudeness? Probably not. More than likely, they would feed off of it and become even more upset.

And now, you're just feeding a cycle that will further anger you and cause rudeness to the next stranger you meet, possibly someone who could use your empathy.

So, the next time you meet a perfect stranger or run into someone at random in a less than ideal situation, consider what they might be going through. Simple empathy and a friendly mind set can make a HUGE difference in your social fortunes.

Get Out Your Social Tool Belt

Humans are problem solvers. We can see a problem, analyze it and develop solutions to that problems using our experience, sometimes instantly. But, if we don't realize there is a problem to be solved or if we grow close minded against potential solutions, things can get a little messy.

It's a pretty cool phenomenon if you think about it, but most people don't think about it and few of us ever take the time to try and solve problems. Instead, we get upset that there is a problem, look for someone else to fix it and then make it worse through negative thoughts.

Sounds pretty ineffective, doesn't it? I could spend half a chapter analyzing why this happens and what psychologists have been saying about our habit of deferring problems through stress, but in reality, all that really matters is that you stop doing it.

The real problem comes in with the way our society works. We create complicated systems with certain people specialized in dealing with those systems. It's all fine and good until something breaks and we need that specialist to make a house call. Then, we start thinking in the same way about our social problems.

Your boyfriend breaks up with you and you think "I wish someone could fix this problem" instead of thinking "what can I do to fix the problem now or in the future?"

You're deferring responsibility for the problem and waiting for a solution to present itself. The easiest path is not to wait for a solution to appear, but to get your hands dirty and create a solution using the tools every one of us has to interact socially.

Keep an Open Mind

To be a likable person, you must keep an open mind – allowing yourself to accept what and who other people are on their terms, not yours. The problem is in how we tend to analyze other people.

We each have a worldview and ideas of "decency" that have been programmed from birth. When someone doesn't fit that worldview, we judge them on a scale of how far from our ideal perspective they fall.

And yet, despite all of that, we've come a long way in recent decades. There once was a time when people would make judgments like this based solely on details of race, gender, religion, or class. Some still do and there is a lot of work left to do.

The key here – don't look at someone different than you and say "I don't like that person because of...." This isn't just a matter of race or religion either.

People do it with almost every personal trait. They see someone who is a different political affiliation and make judgments about their intelligence. They see someone who enjoys a sport or a certain kind of literature and assume they would have nothing of interest to talk about.

Not everyone fits a stereotype – in fact almost no one fits a single stereotype any more. No one is a "country boy" or a "city girl" alone because there are so many influences inundating each of us every day. People are a little bit of everything. And yeah, some people may trend toward one mind set or another, but that doesn't mean you cannot get to know them a bit in turn.

What Do They Do?

People are inherently more interested in a conversation when they can connect on a level beyond general pleasantries. The next time you watch TV, listen for the types of words used to describe products in a commercial.

More than anything, commercials attempt to establish common situations that the highest number of people will relate to. Laundry detergent ads focus on specific situations in which a good detergent is necessary, such as when a grass or food stain sets in. They could just as easily say "we're better", but can anyone connect with that idea?

This comes back to what we talked about in the introduction about other people having a bigger impact on our lot in life than we realize. When someone makes a decision about you, they do so after listening to you, deciding whether to believe you and then measuring their values against yours.

So, when you can create a conversational tone that connects with them on a personal level, they are far more likely to listen to you. Scientists have studied the effect of media and social interaction on our brains, finding that you receive anywhere from 300 to 500 messages every day, trying to persuade you to one or another form of thinking, making your options are severely limited.

That may sound intimidating, but trust me – for us, it's a good thing. It means that you can make yourself instantly more interesting simply by having a wide range of interests in life and learning how to connect with other people.

A little bit later in the book I'm going to talk about how to enhance your skillset so that you tap a boatload of interesting skills when you meet someone new.

But before that, we'll keep it simple with what people are interested in. Specifically, what are you interested in and how can you connect with other people based on those interests?

The number one step to being truly likable is embracing your true interests and then finding people who can connect with you on that level.

Imagine how much easier this process is going to be when you can be yourself and share what you honestly love about life with new people – it will open up new doors that you never even knew existed. You want to showcase your ability to be interesting on your own terms, not someone else's.

Getting to Know their Interests

"Folks are usually about as happy as they make their minds up to be."

— Abraham Lincoln

To be successful in meeting other people, you need to have a wide range of interests and knowledge to draw from.

A well rounded person is a likable person. People are inherently attracted (both socially and sexually) to people with a lot of world experience and knowledge. So no, don't pretend you're not a computer geek, but do try to expand your experiences to include other activities that may come up in conversation.

Just imagine how unfriendly it seems if you're in a conversation and the other person asks you "do you like baseball" and your immediate response is "ugh, no – I'm a gamer myself".

It's rude, unfriendly and pretty much screams to them "leave me alone – I'd rather not talk to anyone who doesn't share my one interest". Is that your intention? Probably not, and so you need to be careful about the message you're sending with your reaction.

The Generosity of Spirit

When you're injured, unhappy, sad, or angry what is the first thing you want?

Someone who cares for you to sit by your side and listen to your concerns, right? Everyone searches for an empathetic ear to listen to your problems can instantly make those problems seem less all-encompassing and help you get on with your life.

So, when trying to be likable, one of your primary goals should be to become that person – the man or woman who can throw all your own worries and concerns out the window and become instantly empathetic to someone else.

Going back to Tim Sanders' book on likability, he labels the four core concepts of likability as friendliness, relevance, empathy, and realness.

We've already discussed how friendliness can have a direct impact on your likability and how to be relevant in someone else's eyes – showcasing talents and interests that will draw their attention. But, empathy is something else entirely. Whereas friendliness and relevance can be achieved by consciously adjusting your social behaviours, empathy comes from within – it needs to be honest and whole and it needs to touch everyone around you, not just the person(s) you're trying to impress.

Honest Empathy

Most people understand what empathy is and why it is so important. We feel it for our spouses and children, for our parents and our pets, but it's much harder to connect with the people you meet every day. We have a habit of filtering out part of the interactions we run into each day and for good reason.

Imagine what happens if you were to be empathetic toward every human being you met. Your life would be torturous. The world is filled with suffering and sadness – it is part of our lot as human beings – so we start filtering out what we "care" about.

But, just because we need to protect ourselves from becoming attached to every living thing we encounter doesn't mean we should ignore opportunities to connect with people on a level beyond simple pleasantries.

There are three steps that can help you build empathy in a conversation as it leads to a new relationship.

Listen

The moment you enter a conversation, the rest of the world should cease to exist. Ignore you mobile phone, don't make eyes at the attractive person near the bar, and let your friends fend for themselves. It's important to give every ounce of your being to every conversation you have. It could be with a salesman at your door, the clerk at a grocery store or a stranger you meet at a networking event. The effect this has is profound. No one puts so much of their energy into a conversation anymore. We're all distracted by our techno-gadgets and our social lives beyond who we're talking to. The simple act of listening will show that you're intrigued and that you care.

React

Don't just listen to the other person talk – react to what they have to say. When someone says something upsetting, show them that you feel their pain. Even if you listen to a conversation 100%, a lack of reaction will make it seem like you're not invested. Fix this through active listening (more in Chapter 5) and generate direct connections with the men and women you meet.

Care

Finally, care about what people have to say. I don't mean "appear to care" about what they have to say, I mean literally care. This is the hardest step in the process because sometimes we just don't care. It sounds callous, but it's true. Someone else's problems are just that – their problems. But, we are human beings and human beings are innately social creatures. We are hard wired to care about each other's problems because that's the only way we can survive as a species. In his book, the Selfish Gene, Richard Dawkins describes how being a "nice guy" doesn't mean you have to finish last. As a part of the "selfish gene" theory, being nice can help you create connections that will allow you to remain healthy and survive potential harm in the future. Caring for someone else propagates physical and mental health and helps everyone to thrive.

The trick is to override that internal voice that says "how does that affect me" by thinking how it would affect you. Imagine someone else's problem as your own. How would you react to it? How would you feel? What would you think or do? These thought exercises will help you immediately invest and engage with someone else's problems and ultimately build an empathetic relationship with them, even if they're a perfect stranger.

Empathy is a powerful tool, but it needs to be sincere. Even moderately faked empathy can come across the wrong way, especially if you let it be known that you're not really paying that much attention.

Imagine what someone would think if you were listening, responding and caring about their problem, only to follow up by taking a phone call and laughing about a movie you and a friend just saw. Your new acquaintance would see right through your "empathy" and probably be further insulted than if you'd just walked away to start with.

Avoiding Sarcasm and Cynicism

It's more and more common for people to respond to situations with cynicism rather than anger these days. It's like a big, humor-filled balloon that cushions our fall when something obnoxious happens. But, it has a nasty side effect of pushing people away at the same time.

Cynicism is like a virus – it spreads – and while your intention may be to show how you don't care any longer about a certain topic like politics or finances, you quickly find that you're making snide comments about everything around you, from the food you order to the person serving it.

So how do you avoid being sarcastic about everything that sets foot in your field of vision? It starts by taking things more seriously. Caring is only the first step – eventually you need to take things seriously as well, because the only way to truly engage a problem you care about is to be part of the solution for someone. Empathy creates a connection; action seals the deal.

The Sarcastic Approach

Someone calls you to offer a switch in your cable or phone service. You let them talk for 5-10 minutes, then start saying snide comments about the process of changing and how cold your dinner has gotten. They finally let you get off the phone and everyone goes their separate way.

The grocery store clerk accidentally drops your eggs on the floor after you've paid for them and in a fluster doesn't even realize it. You grow indignant and demand to see a manager to fix the problem, saying degrading things to her like "nice hands, butterfingers."

Your boyfriend calls and says that he cannot make it to dinner because he needs to meet up with his parents. You call him a momma's boy and tell him he has no guts to stand up to his parents.

An Empathetic Alternative

You calmly explain up front that you're not interested in changing and ask that they remove you from their list. You tell them to have a nice day, understanding that they are just doing a job and likely have enough stress in their life without being yelled at every 5 minutes.

When the clerk drops your eggs on the ground, you help her clean up the mess, ask for new eggs and let her know that it's not a big deal. After making it clear that you'd like them replaced you smile and tell her to have a good day. She feels better and goes on with her work.

When your boyfriend calls about cancelling plans, you ask if you should join him, and when the answer is no, wish him luck. You then call him later than night to find out how the evening went, and explain that he should give you a bit more time when cancelling.

Imagine the difference when you whip out a clever, interesting statement that can make someone laugh or smile instead of just being kind of a jerk, even if it was called for.

This isn't just a tool for meeting new people. Your current boyfriend, friends, and family will all be much happier to spend time with you when they know that you won't blow a gasket every time something goes wrong.

Say More without Speaking

This is where I whip out my Mr Miyagi tips. When you hear "conversation" you think of the words that come out of your mouth, and those words make you nervous.

It's part of being a social wallflower – you don't know what to say or when to say it. But, when you get into that mind-set and start worrying about what you have to say, you end up projecting a lot more than you think.

Consider two guys sitting alone at a party.

One of them is hunched over on the bottom step with his face buried in his phone, trying his hardest to avoid eye contact with the rest of the room. The other one is lounging on a recliner, watching a movie and occasionally smiling as people walk by. Who do you think gets labelled as the loner?

Here's another example:

Two women are sitting in a meeting listening to a presentation by a visiting executive who is interested in starting a new program at their firm. He asks for questions.

One woman has been slouched in her chair, tapping her pen for the last twenty minutes and the other sitting upright, taking notes and making constant eye contact. Both women have questions, but the second will almost certainly be chosen first. Even if you are paying perfect attention and have something interesting to add to the conversation, how you present yourself can have as great an impact on someone as what you say.

People project impressions onto the people they meet constantly and the result is a sort of unspoken conversation. We'll go into this a lot more later when we discuss body language and physical cues, but right now the goal is to avoid being unfriendly in the way you sit, stand or move around other people.

This technique is important not just because it will allow you to generate a more direct impression on the people you meet but because you'll be able to sit and listen to someone without having to actually say anything. They'll see that you're upright, leaning forward, occasionally moving your hands and nodding along and they'll know you're involved. Eye movements, smiles, head gestures and posture all tell a story about your reactions to the story and will help you to showcase your empathy clearly as the story develops.

Exercises and Questions

1. Ask a friend or family member to help you outline at least 5 traits or habits you have that make you appear unfriendly:

2. Spend an entire day imagining the purpose behind the actions of each person you meet. Even if someone is rude to you, ask yourself why you think they were rude and how you would act in the same situation.

3. Start taking notes of the interests your current friends and loved ones have. Look for ways that you can show interest in similar activities, especially with your co-workers. Find ways to engage people you previously didn't spend much time with.

4. Talk to at least two people you have never had a real conversation with and write down three things about each person you did not know today:

5. 5.Write down three things that make you angry on a daily basis (e.g. traffic, telemarketers, your boss) and how you can turn those angry moments into growth moments.

Chapter Three:

The Confidence Machine

"It's kind of fun to do the impossible."

— Walt Disney Company

Read any book about getting along with people – any single book, whether it be about dating, getting ahead at work, or just making friends – and you'll find one common trait on top of the list.

The single most important trait is confidence and it always will be.

Unfortunately, when you're not confident in your social abilities, you'll start thinking things like "what if I say the wrong thing" or "what does he think about me?"

So, to fully detach your conversations and interactions from the constant connection to yourself, you need to be confident.

You should look good, feel good and know for a fact that everything you say is 100% what you think and believe – there should be no regrets.

If someone doesn't like what you say or do, you should feel confident enough to move on quickly, learning from any mistakes you make and pushing to the next interaction.

That's hard. Actually, it's extremely hard and it's also why so many people skip this step completely. They read books about how to dress, stand, and talk and yet they forget how important it is to overhaul how they *think* about pretty much everything.

This is exactly where we're going to start and it should be an important part of your likability plan from the ground up.

Improving Yourself

I don't care what your goal is; if you look messy and therefore feel unattractive you're going to have a hard time boosting your confidence. I don't mean "unattractive" in the manner that other people don't innately find you appealing. I mean dirty, unkempt, or generally messy – the things that you can change with relative ease and just haven't.

The last thing I want to do is put a dent in your self-esteem when trying to improve it, but we need to start somewhere, so I need you to be 100% honest with yourself.

Do you look and feel as good as you want to? Or are there things you'd like to polish up? This is a tricky subject area, because I wholeheartedly feel that no one person needs to change who they are to meet others.

However, I *do* feel that the human body is an advertisement for how we feel about ourselves. When you see someone wearing ratty tennis shoes with dirt under their nails, faded clothes, and uncut hair, what do you think? It's probably that the person in front of you doesn't think very highly of themselves and treats their body accordingly.

Not only does it affect how other people see you, it affects how you see yourself. When you get dressed up in your finest clothes, fix your hair, take a shower, and step out, you probably feel a lot better about yourself, at least on a subconscious level. It's a natural reaction.

So, a big part of your confidence boosting is developing good habits and activities that will help you honestly feel better about yourself.

Taking Care of Your Body and Mind

Step one is to take better care of yourself. This may not affect every reader, but I'll wager a guess that most of you have at least a partial tendency to become lazy in this area of your life. And if you're aiming to improve your likability so you can meet someone of the opposite sex, this is even more important.

I like to keep it simple and I recommend you do the same. Why spend thousands of dollars when you could spruce things up a bit and back the package up with an interesting person on the inside. That's our goal, remember. I'm not trying to whitewash the real you. I just want to polish it up for presentation.

Hair – Hair simply needs to be taken care of. You don't need a $100 hair cut or a fancy wave in it to impress people. But, ratty, overly long, untrimmed hair isn't going to work. Keep your hair well-kept and trim any unsightly bodily hair as often as possible.

Clothing – Wear clothing appropriate for the situation. Going to a party for work? Wear something spiffy and professional. Going to a beach to relax? Get a new swimsuit. Your style is entirely up to you, but make sure your clothing is clean, appropriate, and refreshing to look at.

Scent – I don't recommend pouring on the perfume or cologne unless you know what you're doing, but at the very least get some deodorant and a nice body wash to cover up any unsightly odours that might arise while dancing or going about your work on a hot day.

Feet – If you're wearing shoes, polish those puppies up and keep them in shape. When the shoes start to tear, rip, or fall apart, replace them. If you wear anything open toed, go the extra mile and really clean up those piggies.

Hands – Same deal. Use some moisturizer to keep your hands decently soft (at least comfortable to shake), trim your nails and keep them clean every day.

Fitness – Weight is not important. It really isn't. But fitness can make a difference. This means the ability to walk a couple miles without feeling exhausted. You should be able to keep up with anyone you meet. Not only does fitness help you feel better about yourself, it will help you physically and emotionally feel better – a huge plus when trying to go into conversations with a positive mind set. Try a new cardio class you've been wanting to take, like spin (which can help you burn up to 1,000 calories in a fifty minute workout!) or a dance class that will allow you to have fun while blasting fat.

Your body is your temple, so treat it well. Focus on a fun workout because working out will hardly feel like a work out when you're dancing, or swimming your heart out! (aim to exercise for at least 3 days a week for 30 or more minutes.) Preferably, exercise 6 days a week and get your heart rate up with aerobic exercise. Not only will it get your body into fighting shape, it will help you feel so much better about who you are, what you want, and what you attract into your life.

Chapter Four:

Learning New Skills

"It isn't what you have or who you are or where you are or what you are doing that makes you happy or unhappy. It is what you think about it."

— Dale Carnegie, How to Win Friends and Influence People

For decades, scientists have been uncovering how certain foods, like sugar, excess fat, and artificial additives can cause vitamin depletion that leads to depression and unhappiness.

Eat well, take care of your body and you'll feel better both physically and emotionally. And when you feel better emotionally, you'll become physically healthier. Once you get into this powerful cycle, you'll be ready to take on life with renewed vigour.

What should you eat? There are a lot of foods to choose from, but generally speaking, the fewer preservatives, fats, sugars, and salts in the foods you consume, the better.

Aim for non-processed foods, plenty of raw fruits and vegetables, and plenty of whole grains. Trust me – you will *feel* so much better when you take this step to feed your body what it really needs and desires.

Learning New Skills

Next up we have skills – that library of cool things you can do that other people wish they could. Without a good base of skills, you'll start comparing yourself to people in ways that just plain isn't healthy. It's a bad habit to start with, but if you don't have anything to show off and feel confident about, it can be hard to overcome that constant, nagging feeling that you're just not as good as the people you hang out with.

The solution is simple – learn some new skills. Get out there and learn how to do things that will make you infinitely more interesting and confident in your abilities. I'm generalizing a lot here, but for good reason.

You can literally learn how to do anything and draw interest from the people you meet. The key here is diversity, not outrageousness.

1. What Are You Good At Already?

Ask yourself what you already excel at.

There should be something that you do better than the people you know or that you have always been very good at. Pinpoint that special activity or skillset and find ways to increase it.

If you're a good runner, get out there and play a sport with a lot of running like Soccer or Basketball – you'll have something more interesting to talk about with anyone who plays those sports and other athletes in general.

If you love to sing, head over to your local bar on karaoke night and sing your heart out!

If you love to paint, write or draw, designate one day of the week to devote to your hobby. The more you focus on things you love, the more love you can bring into your life, simply because you're auto-magnetizing people to you.

The truth is, people are drawn to others who are energized, passionate and happy. The more you focus on what you love to do, the greater you'll be able to attract others to you.

2. Learn How to Describe Your Skills

When you meet someone, it's easy to be excited about what you can now do, but introducing it should be done in a way that draws them into conversation – not through bragging.

People love to share what they think and help you succeed in your endeavours. Don't cut them off when they try to add to the conversation. Just because you develop a skillset doesn't mean you're an expert who can walk around telling people what to believe or think about it.

There are so many different types of skills and personal development opportunities out there. Just to give you an idea of how interesting of a person you can become, here are a few of my favourites:

Learn a Language – Learning a language is one of the most effective ways to meet new people. Not only do you open yourself up to an entire world of individuals who don't speak your native tongue, you will meet other people trying to learn whatever language you're interested in. Plus, it is a nice addition to your resume.

Play a Sport – Physical activity is good for more than just skill development. It keeps you active, helps you feel good about yourself, and lets you show off how skilled you can be with a synthetic ball (or how funny you can be when you fall on your butt). Sports are one of the greatest ways to meet people, even if you're trying to find a date, and the skills you develop can be applied to pretty much anything else you enjoy.

Read About a Topic – Reading is not a good way to meet people directly, but it does build up a nice knowledge base that can be tapped in conversation. If you've ever been trapped in a dull, dragging conversation with someone who doesn't know the difference between the President of France and George Clooney, you know that having at least a basic pool of knowledge will make you infinitely more interesting to people you've just met.

Write a Book or Poetry – Writing is a fantastic way to grow your skills. While I don't usually recommend going around showing off your poetry knowledge (quoting poetry to people repeatedly will usually come across as condescending at best), simply being agile with the pen makes you more effective in communicating ideas to other people – in email, in conversation or over the phone.

Go Camping or Hiking – Roughing it in the great outdoors opens up a number of doors to those willing to go through them. Hiking and camping aren't for everyone, but venturing outdoors can provide you with a lot of fun things to do on the weekend. Also, meeting fellow outdoorsy people is incredibly easy once you get into the swing of things. **Learn How to Paint or Craft** – If you'd like to develop more aesthetic skills, painting or crafting in the comfort of your home can be a fantastic way to develop a connection with the texture and feel of your world. Even non-artistic types can go down this road with model car kits or electronics kits.

Build Things in Your Garage – Want to be the talk of the neighbourhood? Fire up that mitre saw and start putting together dog houses, fences, and patios in your garage. People will gravitate to those who are constantly building and creating. It's a part of the human nature to be curious about those who can create.

Learn to Play an Instrument – An instrument is an instant conversation starter. And while some instruments are harder than others to learn, you can pick up a guitar for less than $100 at a pawn shop and learn how to pick out some basic tunes in your spare time with an hour a day of practice.

Learn to Cook – Cooking is fun, popular, and incredibly healthy for you if done right. Being able to talk about food, offer recipes, and discuss your recent concoctions can generate a huge opening in conversation too.

Study Plants and Gardening – Gardening is relaxing and offers plenty of opportunities to learn more about the natural world. Don't think people will talk about gardening with you? Think again.

Fix Up Your Home – Home repair and improvement is a fun way to get out and use your hands. It also offers you a way to once again attract attention in your neighbourhood and build up your reputation.

If you're looking to make new friends and have something interesting to say, take a stab at any one of the things on this list, or better yet, go out there and look for an interest that matches your personality.

Literally anything works for this – it just takes the right dedication to make it happen.

Self-Image and Self Talk

What do you do about those obnoxious voices? How do we shut them up for good, or better yet, replace them with positive voices that can encourage us through even the toughest social encounters?

Through positive imaging and self-talk.

For as long as I've been an adult, I've practiced Mind Power exercises that tap into the innate ability we all have to talk ourselves into an optimistic outlook on life. And the best part is that it's actually as simple as it sounds.

Here's the idea.

Our brains are very powerful, very intricate machines, but they can only handle so much "reality". So, if the world around us is significantly different than how we perceive it, our brains will try to close the gap and make things match up to how they seem.

It's called cognitive dissonance and self-starters have been using it for centuries to create a positive mind set and make seemingly impossible goals come true.

Boosting Self Esteem

Confidence is built on a firm foundation of self-esteem.

You have to feel good about yourself before you can honestly say to yourself "anything is possible" and better yet, display that confidence to a perfect stranger.

But, self-esteem is as notoriously tough trait to regain when life has battered you around of late.

It's one of those things that come as much out of your environment as from within. It's incredibly hard to feel good about yourself if you're surrounded by people who constantly tell you how silly what you're doing is or try to make you feel bad about yourself. So, to combat that kind of thinking, you'll need to make a few changes.

Creating a Positive Mind Set

Positivity. It's a simple word but it's one of the most powerful things you'll learn in this book. You can't just wake up one day and go buy positivity like you would a new wardrobe.

You can't have your negative energy cut off like a mop of shaggy hair. You have to build it from within, generating sincere, positive power deep inside that your body can thrive on.

When you wake up each day, remind yourself of the positive influences in your world and the opportunities you have, things open up – you'll feel a surge of energy unlike anything you've ever encountered before.

Here are some additional exercises inspired by the exercises used by the US Nursing Association to help patients recover from disease and surgery. For years the power of positive thinking has been shown to help in healing and achieving success:

Use Positive Words When Talking – Focus on saying things in positive ways, even when describing a negative situation. It will help you to think of solutions and better yet understand what other people's actions are caused by.

Repeat Your Affirmations Daily – Get those affirmations in place and repeat them day after day. Once you feel an affirmation has taken hold, find new ones and continue to improve yourself.

Direct Thoughts to Positive Imagery – Images and visualization have a profound impact on how we think. Shift your mind set from negative words to positive images, even if those images are not related to what you're trying to do.

Forgive Yourself for Mistakes Made – The past is a fickle mistress who will come back to haunt you time and again. Instead of worrying about the effects of what has come before, forgive yourself and learn to live your life in the present.

Visualize Negative Thoughts Turning into Positive – Here's an activity that works wonders for negative thoughts. When you have a negative though, visualize it in your head and then slowly transition it into a positive image instead. Just got a parking ticket? Visualize it paid off and torn up. You still have to pay that ticket, but now you're thinking of the time after, not the act of paying.

Create an Ideal Image and Work Toward It – This is a common NLP (neuro-linguistic programming) exercise. In it, you visualize your ideal self – the perfect version of you that you want to present to people. Then, you visualize yourself as you currently see yourself and slowly work toward shifting your mental image of one or two things at a time to the ideal self. For example, if you're worried about your weight, you would visualize your ideal weight and your current weight and then slowly change how you think of yourself to be closer and closer to that ideal image.

List Reasons You Will Be Successful – Write a list of ways and reasons you will find success in your life. Be as specific as possible.

Surround Yourself with Positivity – Find ways to surround yourself with positive energies. Images on your computer, tapes with affirmations on them, and books with positive messages will help you stay positive.

Track Your Thoughts and Review them Later – Write down your thoughts as they occur to you every day in a notebook and then come back to them later to review what you were thinking and better yet, why. This works because you can identify negative thoughts at a later date and determine if they were necessary.

Eliminate Self Criticism – Stop digging at yourself internally. Consider whether you've made a good decision or not and then move on. Think of ways to do better in the future, not to bash on yourself in the past.

Remove Negative Influences – If someone says negative things to you or if you're surrounded by negative reinforcement, get away from it.

Share with Friends or a Professional – Find someone you can share both your negative and positive thoughts with. This can be a close friend, a spouse, or even a counsellor that you would talk to on a regular basis.

Be Nice to Others – This one is simple. Be nice to other people and you'll feel more positive about yourself. Displaying negativity can create negative thoughts and cause you to continue displaying negativity going forward.

Find Inspiring Input in Books, Movies, or Poetry – Find quotes, movies, music or other mediums that provide you inspiration. Keep them close by and review them when you need a boost.

There are many more ways you can sit down right now and create a mind-set that is more positive, more engaged and generally more interested in being successful, but it takes time.

This is just a starter list – something that will help you start thinking of the world in terms of what will help you find success.

But, it takes dedication.

Positivity is harder for some than others. Many of us have been living in an if-then world for too long. We think, "If this happens, then I'm stuck dealing with that."

Start thinking in terms of when-will. For you, the balance of your life should be based on "when something happens, I will make something better happen". It's a powerful, affirmative attitude and it will help you remain positive even in the face of the worst possible situations.

Reduce Negative Influences

While creating a positive mind set, it's time to cut out all the negativity that we tend to dwell on in our lives.

Some of it is internal, and you'll find that the more positive you become, the less negative thoughts will plague your days, but all those unsavoury influences outside of you can put a serious dent in your new perspective if you're not careful.

So, you need to take a scalpel to the relationships that make you feel worst.

If you have friends that constantly tell you how you cannot do something, or are in a romantic relationship with someone who doesn't support any of your hobbies or dreams, you either need to sit down and have a chat about or you need to completely remove them from your life.

There a lot of situations where negativity can dig in and ruin your world view. But, that doesn't mean you cannot find success in those situations.

You must learn to either remove those influences or give them less stock. When it is family or a loved one, you should communicate your desire to hear positive support, and if you cannot, limit the contact you have to ensure you are more successful.

Find Like Minded People

Once the negativity is cut out of your life, it's time to replace it with people who get you. Lucky for you there is a whole book sitting in front of you that can help you do just that.

This comes with time, but I want you to honestly consider every time you meet someone for the first time what that person brings to your life.

Avoid selfishly thinking about what they can do for you – that's a habit no one should get into. Instead, think about how their attitude will affect your self-esteem and general approach to the world.

If they're constantly positive and honestly enjoy your company, they're a good friend to have. If they complain a lot and put you down, think about whether you really need to be friends with someone who makes you feel crummy.

Stress Reduction 101

Right up there with negativity, stress can put a huge drain on your likability. Imagine what someone would think if they met you right after you finished working a 12 hour day, running errands and sitting in traffic for another hour. Would they be very interested in your new kickboxing hobby or would they think "man, they are *stressed!*."

The last thing you want is for stress to become a leading trait that defines the impression you make on others. It can make you cranky and generally unfriendly.

So, before stress gets as stranglehold on your social life, we're going to do a little surgery on your cortisol output and calm you down with some simple, age old exercises.

Meditation

First up, there is the idea of physical extrication from stress.

If you exercise daily as I recommended a few page ago, you're on a good path already. But, beyond simple fitness, you should take advantage of simple breathing exercises and meditation – one of civilization's oldest and most effective stress reduction tools.

There are many types of meditation, but I have always found peace and relaxation in the simplest of Buddhist breathing exercises.

The idea is simple. You relax, push away the worries of the day and give yourself enough time to focus on the one thing that matters most – "you".

Set Aside a Time Every Day –

Meditation is most powerful when it becomes a standard part of your day. When your mind knows for a fact that you'll be given the same 30+ minutes every day to relax and detach from all the stressful influences you've managed to accumulate, it will fall into a much greater state of relaxation.

Sit in a Comfortable Position

How you meditate is really up to you, but personally I prefer to sit in a full lotus, with both feet curled beneath my legs into a cross legged position. You can also use a half lotus, placing one foot against the inside of your opposite thigh. Sitting is best for me because it allows me to focus only on the breathing exercise, not the act of walking. Lying down works for some people as well, but I tend to get sleepy, so I stay upright.

Breathe Deeply

Once you have relaxed into a comfortable sitting position, breathe deeply through your nose. Pull the air slowly into your lungs, following the flow of the air into your nose, through your throat and into your lungs. Your diaphragm and stomach should sleep where less air is needed. Keep doing this process over and over again, following those breaths into your body time and again.

expand with each breath, filling you up like a balloon. Hold the breath for half a second and then release it, slowly letting the air seep out of your nose or mouth. The longer you breathe, the longer you should hold that breath. A relaxed body uses less oxygen and can relax into a state closer to

Focus on that Breath Carefully

The key to meditation, especially for newcomers to the exercise, is to choose a single focal point and pour all of your energy into it. In this case, that focal point is your breathing. The steady flow of life force into and out of your body should funnel your consciousness deeper into your body as you fall into a steady meditation. One thing many people will do is focus on a point on their body – a single position in their head, throat, chest or abdomen that they can feel the breath going through. The lower the point, the further you will fall into a meditative trance.

The Flow of Thoughts

In a meditative state, the free flow of thoughts is a normal part of the process. Your brain will allow thoughts to come and go as they please. It is okay for this to happen. The more you try to force your thoughts to stop, the more forceful they will become and the harder it will be for you to relax. So, instead of trying to force your thoughts to stop, let them flow. You are a rock in a stream bed and your thoughts are the current. As they pass over you, they become part of you, but only for a moment. The next moment, they are out of sight, beyond your concern as another one works its way toward you.

This exercise, as simple as it sounds, is the very method used for centuries by some of the most enlightened bodies that ever lived to detach from the constant influx of worries and stressors in life. If you feel yourself losing the constant battle against stress, meditation can help equalize your strengths and overcome that feeling that you're losing it.

Goal Keeping and Strength Development

Another easy way to cut down on stress is to outline and visualize all of your goals and strengths on paper (or e-paper as the case may be).

One of the leading causes of stress is scheduling. You have too much to do and don't feel like there is enough time in the day to complete it all.

So, instead of pushing yourself to the limit and then feeling inadequate for not getting it done, step back and think "what can I really get done today?""?

Goal Tracking – Number one on the list; keep track of the goals you have from day to day. Be realistic about how much you can get done from one moment to the next, and use goal setting software to create an outline of your day's necessities. Every goal you set should have actionable tasks you can complete, and specific tools you can use to generate successful results.

Develop Strengths – Everyone is good at some things more than others. Human beings are unique in every way from each other and therefore are able to do things that others cannot. If you're not an athlete, you learned in school early that you should focus your energies on something more suited to your talents – academics, creativity, or something more immediately practical like shop. The same is true in your adulthood. Relax and find a way to recognize and then replicate your strengths in every part of your life.

Automate and Relax – Put it on autopilot and watch as your world becomes infinitely easier to manipulate and remain relaxed at the same time. Outsource tasks you don't have time to complete, delegate tasks at work, ask for help at home – whatever you need to do, ask yourself if there is a faster, more efficient way to do it. If there is, you'll save a tremendous amount of time and make your life infinitely easier.

Stress is a natural part of your life. It always will be.

When your child breaks their arm or you lose hours at work, you *will* be stressed out about it. It's only natural. But, when you're able to sit back and relax – understanding the purpose of that stress and why it is unnecessary, life becomes a lot easier, and you become a much more likable person to be around.

Exercises and Questions

1. Sit down and write up five of your strengths and three ways
   for each strength to be encouraged and improved upon:

2. Create a list of 3-5 skills you can work on immediately.

3. Keep a log of your actions toward those skills on daily basis.
   I recommend working on one skill at a time and developing
   an hour a day to the development of your skills in that field.

4. Create a list of 3-5 affirmations that you can repeat to yourself every day for the next 90-120 days.

5. Analyze the people in your life right now. Make a list of the people who are a positive influence and all those who are a negative influence. Determine if you can spend more time with the former and less with the latter.

6. Set aside at least 20-30 minutes a day in which you can meditate or exercise and develop a more successful approach to your problems.

7. Start tracking your goals by writing down at least 5 of them
    that you'd like to complete in the next 4 months.

Chapter Five:

How Other People See You

"Do not go where the path may lead, go instead where there is no path and leave a trail."

— Ralph Waldo Emerson

I honestly don't care what other people think of me, but that doesn't mean I don't work to put on an affable, likable coat of armour whenever I go into public.

You may not realize you do it, you may even deny you do it, but I'm here to tell you that almost every judgment you make of your fellow human beings is driven by their body language. It's a part of who we are, even when we don't realize it.

So, when you want to be likable, you need to *look, talk and act like a likable person.* Don't worry; I'm not going to give you makeover and tell you to just "be comfortable" in

those new clothes.

We're going to go through specific body language cues and how you can shift your interactions with people so they see someone who is confident, cool, and most of all, likable.

Why Body Language Matters

I've rambled on a few times now about how important body language is, but what does that actually mean?

We know my dog would get upset when I grew angry, but what about other people and what exactly do they notice?

Body language is nothing new. This isn't a secret that someone just discovered five years ago and we're just now uncovering the full extent of. It's been around since before written or spoken language and it's a fundamental part of who we are as human beings.

People were grunting, shaking their heads and standing up to show off their dominance to one another when they were still batting each other with sticks – and while a lot of the context has been lost in the last few hundred thousand years, we still say a lot with our bodies.

The people who can catch on to the subtleties of body language and reciprocate the conversation are the ones that do best in social situations.

To illustrate my point, go into any bar or club and try to have a detailed conversation with someone. Can they even hear everything you're saying? Eventually the goal is to separate a romantic interest from the herd and talk to them in a quieter setting, but at the outset, you'll notice that there are too many distractions for a strictly verbal conversation.

So you have to lean in, open your body language, smile and laugh to make sure they know you're interested. Without the common signs of romantic interest, where would you be? Alone in that bar, that's where.

How People Read You

You're an open book.

If we were talking in person right now, I'd know more about you than you'd feel comfortable saying, and you're broadcasting it to everyone you meet.

But, what exactly do people see when they watch you? Is it the cool confidence of someone without anything to hide, or a nervous, uncomfortable person unsure of their place in the world?

How other people see you will have a pretty big impact on how likable you are, but I don't want you to think about that just yet. In fact, stop thinking about it at all.

Body language is not something you can consciously control – at least not in the long run. It's a learned behaviour, like walking or riding a bike. You'll do it automatically, reflecting your internal state.

There's a good reason we talked about confidence and internal states before body language – it will set the table for you to actually sit there with your arms open and your smile bright and inviting.

So, until you're capable of actually feeling comfortable in the company of complete strangers, you'll need to work on a few specific body language hot spots that will help you *feel* more confident and in control of a situation.

Eventually, your brain will pick it up and run with it, making your life much easier.

What Not to Do

Bad body language is everywhere. Walk into any crowded room and look for someone slumped in their chair or with their arms and legs crossed up. Do they look inviting or do they look bored and closed off?

When you walk into the cafeteria at work, are you more likely to talk to the guy staring at his sandwich with his shoulders hunched over or the woman who is smiling genially at the cashier with straight posture, while looking you in the eye?

It's a pretty simple distinction, but we almost never think about it. But when you do, you'll realize just how different bad body language makes you look to other people.

Example A:

Tim has a job interview with a big firm that does exactly what he's always wanted to do. As a salesman, he's sold a lot of things in his life that he wasn't proud of, but Company A sells an automobile that he is proud of and he wants to be part of that process. When he arrives at the job interview, though, Tim is uncomfortable and nervous. He walks into the interview with sweaty palms, grows even more unsure of himself and then proceeds to grow weary of the situation in which he has just put himself. He keeps his head down, doesn't make eye contact, has his arms crossed and hunches forward slightly in his chair, almost as though he has a stomach ache. The interviewer sees this discomfort, and despite a glowing resume and references, puts Tim on the 'maybe' pile. Salesmen can't be nervous in high pressure situations – Tim likely won't get that job.

Tim's problem is that he put too much of himself into the prospect of getting that job. In his head, he couldn't help but imagine already having the position, and as a result, he starts to worry about what will happen when he *doesn't* get it. He grows nervous, then protective and hides himself behind his body gestures. The result is a blown interview and a huge mistake on Tim's part.

Example B:

Jill broke up with her boyfriend three months ago and finally feels ready to step out and meet a new guy. Her friends drag her to nail salon, buy her a new dress and get hour to a club on a Friday night, if nothing else to get her back out in the dating

scene. At first, Jill has fun, but as the night wears on, she starts to think of her ex- boyfriend and so, when men look at her across the crowded room, she frowns and looks away. At first, it's unconscious, but soon she realizes it and feels embarrassed that she has been pushing people away. As the night goes on, one or two men come over to talk to Jill, but her quietness, closed body language and perpetual frown push them away before they have a chance to truly get into a real conversation.

Jill's cold behaviour is due in part to the fact that she is distracted by memories that make her uncomfortable. The memory of her last relationship leaves an imprint on her mind that manifests in her body language. Guys see that closed, uninviting stance and most of them don't even give it a shot. Others try and are quickly treated to what appears as a cold, uninterested woman. While Jill may not be ready to date just yet, she is also embarrassed by how unfriendly she is being without even realizing why.

Bad body language happens for a lot of reasons, and 99% of the time we don't realize what we're doing. Any of the following can cause someone to grow uncomfortable and distance themselves from others:

Anger – When mad, people tend to spend a lot of time repeating thoughts and running through scenarios internally. Our bodies reflect that emotional state and it doesn't look pretty.

Discomfort – Discomfort displays in a number of ways, usually in protective, standoffish gestures that are designed to put distance between you and the source of your discomfort. **Nervousness** – When nervous you may fidget, sweat, and become flustered in conversation. Nervousness doesn't go away with body language control, but at least other people won't realize it's there.

94

Tiredness or Hunger – When tired, we tend to lose control of most of our outward controls. We grow lumpy and sometimes grouchy. Hunger can make this worse. When going to meet people or involving in social situations, make sure you're rested and satiated.

Distraction – Distraction manifests in a lack of eye contact, distant voice, non- squared posture and general disinterest.

Stress – Stress manifests in almost every way we've discussed. That's because stress is a combination of nervousness, discomfort and sometimes anger – so much so that it can take over and dictate a conversation.

Basically, when we feel bad inside, our body reflects that on the outside. The solution is simple – do everything in your power to feel good on the inside and your body will take care of the rest, displaying your generally happy demeanour for anyone you meet.

Let's Look at Your Body

Pretty much, you need to change every little thing about how you carry yourself and approach the people you meet. Heck, even the friends and family members you see on a regular basis would probably benefit from open, inviting body language.

So, let's take a look at what you can do right now to make a big difference in how you look to the people around you.

Eye Contact

Eye contact immediately tells someone a lot about who you are, what you expect out of a conversation and much more. Think about it.

When you look at someone and they immediately turn their eyes away, you know instantly that they are shy or trying to hide something. How you interpret that depends on a lot of other circumstances, but you know a lot about their internal state by the flicker of their eyes.

It works in both directions. If you want to be read in a certain way, you need to use eye contact to your benefit. Look people in the eye when you want to get their attention, smile - David Duncan (www.hodu.com)

when you want to show them you're interested in talking and look away when you'd rather not discuss something.

Smiling

The human smile is a singularly expressive gesture matched by only a handful of other members of the animal kingdom. With the flex and twinge of our facial muscles we can display hundreds of emotions instantly to anyone we meet.

I generally recommend that you smile at everyone you meet as much as possible. Don't smile constantly, but rather when it is called for in a conversation or after an interesting or funny comment, but also avoid sombre, frowning looks.

Posture

Stand straight up and hold your body in a position that will convey strength and power to the people you meet.

Hold your shoulders back, your neck up, your back straight and keep your gestures open and inviting. Not only is there a subconscious link to the idea of "power" that we translate as confidence, but you'll look more interesting and engaging than if you were curled up in a ball.

People who hunch over with shoulders down and head pointed at the ground look sicklier than they do friendly – it doesn't work to engage people in conversation.

96

Arms and Legs

Open body language is one of the most powerful tools for conveying your intentions to a room packed with strangers. And your arms and legs are the fulcrums of this conversation. If you hold your arms crossed over you abdomen, the message is that of discomfort.

You're trying to close up and hold back. Instead, keep your body language open and most of all relaxed to convey that you're interested in what's being said at all times.

Your Stride

Walking is another very powerful indicator of strength in a conversation.

When people see you walk they will gauge a lot about your personality. If you walk too quickly, you'll appear to be nervous and in a hurry. If you walk too slowly or too erratically you appear unfocused or drunk.

So, you should work to relax, stand straight and walk smoothly, without rushing any movements.

How You Sit

The body does many things when sitting.

It's an unnatural position, and therefore those without the strength or experience in sitting properly tend to slouch, stoop, or bend over in ways that are less than flattering.

To end the messages sent through these poor sitting habits, consciously sit straight up, hold your shoulders back and keep your arms and legs unfolded.

By maintaining a careful and open stance, your body will appear open and you will appear powerful and healthy. If you're uncomfortable sitting like this, consider some core strengthening exercises to boost the strength around your abdomen and lower back.

Those Nervous Twitches

Everyone has nervous twitches that get them into trouble. I used to rub salt from potato chips and sandwiches on my shoulder without realizing it. This bad habit actually killed a date for me back in college and probably put off a number of other people without me realizing it. Other nervous twitches I've seen people suffer from include:

Shaky Legs – You know that up and down stutter of a knee under the table? It's distracting and sometimes a little unnerving, especially during calm, relaxed conversation.

Licking or Biting Lips – While you may be doing something unintentionally, any movement around your lips can be taken the wrong way, especially if you're talking to someone of the opposite sex. Avoid unintentional lip bites or licks to keep the conversation in the right quadrant.

Biting Nails or Picking Nose – Anything that someone else might consider gross should be brought under control as soon as possible. This includes belching, scratching, gum

chewing, and whatever else you can think of that is less than attractive to most people.

Frowning or Grimacing – Some people make facial gestures in response to a thought they're having in their head. That's a dangerous game to play. If someone sees you across the room frowning in their direction, they may think you don't want to talk to them, when in reality you may just be thinking of a TV show you saw the night before. Try to control your facial gestures as well as possible.

The list goes on and on.

Remember one thing about nervous twitches and tics. Not all of them are controllable. If you honestly cannot control a tic that is interfering with your social life, it may be necessary to seek professional help or consultation to discuss possible treatment.

And if the tic isn't overly distracting, consider just telling someone when you meet them in a joking way that you have a nasty habit of accidentally kicking their chair. They'll find it funny and you can move on from there.

Now, Let's Read Other People

I always start with a look at my body language for a good reason. It makes it so much easier to read what someone else is saying with a casual toss of their hair or crossed arms. Take everything we just talked about and apply it to a random stranger you run into at the cafeteria.

What would your first response be to someone with their arms crossed and eyes down – they probably don't want to talk.

Now, if they opened up and smiled in your direction, you'd take it as an invitation of sorts to at least say hi, right? As simple as it seems, reading other people is one of the hardest parts of body language.

Why?

Because, we're so focused on ourselves and the impression our bodies are making. While you're busy checking if you're sitting straight or watching for someone's attention, you could completely ignore a potential friend who smiles in your direction.

It's a complicated process, but the sooner you master your own body language, the sooner you'll be able to easily digest what other people are doing.

You can easily read other people's body language and know how to immediately respond perfectly—so that you drastically reduce the tricky social blunders to a minimum—with my *body motion mechanism.*

Your *body motion mechanism technique* is about tweaking the way you sit, stand and even smile, so that you can receive the kind of response you want from others.

In other words, you can stand next to someone as they talk (with your arms crossed across your chest) and deal with stubbornness, the inability to persuade them to close the deal, or the response of negativity or you can stand next to them (with your arms by your side), smiling, nodding in empathy, and making solid eye contact – all of which promotes a sense of trust and connection and persuade them to agree to what you're asking, respond in a positive manner and even extend themselves to you for the future!

You can do this all without saying a thing. It's that powerful!

In order to do the body motion mechanism technique, you simply mirror the body language of the person you're interacting with.

The whole idea is when your body language mirrors theirs, you convey connection, trust, understanding, sympathy and a sense of belonging. When you don't mirror their body language, you can convey something much different, and any of the following: pessimism, boredom, complacency, distrust, and negativity.

Who would you rather hire for a job, or enthusiastically want to go out on a date with—the person with crossed arms and who avoids eye contact with you, or the one who smiles, nods while I talk, and looks at me in the eye (instead of being distracted while she's speaking to me)?

Practice the body motion mechanism technique by copying what another person does, as they are talking to you.

If you're sitting side by side, notice their angle. Are their legs turned in towards yours? If so, mimic them by doing the same. Are they smiling? Smile back. Are they looking at you while speaking or listening to you? Look back at them. Sit up straight, with your shoulders rolled back and your back straight (this convey confidence, and confident people as you know by now, are popular people.)

You truly do have more control than you think you do.

The power of popularity is in your hands. Make others gravitate towards you simply by mimicking something they're already doing! When you mimic their body language, you'll become someone who instantly becomes trustworthy, caring and magnetizing (the recipe for lifelong likeability!)

Command a Room and Gain a Following (No Matter Who You're Speaking To)

If you remember from the introduction of this book, I told you that people aren't born inherently likeable. It's a learned ability.

But luckily, after you finish reading this book and by placing extra attention to this chapter, you'll become someone who HAS learned it—and learned it well!

Anyone who is popular isn't just kind, fun to be around and confident. They aren't just unique in some way or another, or empathetic towards others. They actually are highly skilled at commanding a crowd—and gaining the attention and admiration of others.

This section will dive into several techniques you can begin using today in order to achieve just that.

One of the most important techniques you'll learn about in my program is what's known as the *command principle*.

The *command principle* is about having such an intense likeability that people hang on your every word. If you think about Oprah, what's the first word that comes into your mind? Rich? Charismatic? Intelligent? Captivating?

If you agree with any of those words, well, you'd be right. She has the power to say anything—and no matter what she says, you'll hear the audience (or maybe yourself mutter), "Yep, totally right." Even if she's not saying something that's mind blowing, *it's still blowing your mind.*

She practices the command principle to a 'T', and in fact, she's mastered it.

In fact, any great leader has and continues to do so. The command principle is about walking into any room boldly, pausing before you speak, and asserting yourself as an authoritarian. Here's how to nail it:

Walk in assertively. This is a tried and true body language trick to convey confidence that you'll see every powerful, popular and success person do (no matter what their sex may be.) Command respect and admiration simply by walking as though your audience has been waiting their entire life to see you.

Pause. This step is simple. Once you've gotten all eyes on you, pause for about five seconds. Build the suspense so people are on the edge of their chair as to what to expect. **Assert yourself as an expert.** There are two things that people really love, no matter what nationality they may come from or what race they may be. People love a leader who is an expert in something they are not, and someone who comes across as humble. You can achieve both of these traits in one swift swoop—and when you do, you'll get people to listen and respond favourably to you in an instant. First, in order to assert yourself as an expert, you have to treat yourself that way. Stand up straight.

Tell yourself you're an expert (expert writer, expert salesperson, expert marketer, whatever it may be).

There's power in repetition, and the more you tell yourself what you are (even if it seems ridiculous), the more you'll believe in that very thing you want to become— and emulate it to the world.

Don't be shy about telling people what you're good at. You can come across as humble (the only thing that all people love) by coming across as a student of life.

Oprah does this very well. She's always nodding and smiling (whether she's interviewing a legendary blues singer or a single mom who's endured some rough breaks). She repeats what's she learned, and says, "I love that."

Because she comes across as a humble, self-proclaimed 'student of life,' she continues to captivate people with whatever she says. You can do the same by mimicking her!

The *loyal sidekick hook* is all about building an army of supporters to have your back, be on your team and stay loyal to you for a lifetime. Every great leader in the world has applied the loyal sidekick hook, and they still do (although now it's just become a habit.) Here's how to generate a devoted following in a heartbeat:

Whether you want to have stronger supporters in your work life or social life, you can do it by showing interest in others. People respond to generosity. Like a said before, we are selfish beings for the most part.

In relationships, we may focus (accidentally) on what we're getting, instead of what we're giving. We do what we need to do to 'work our way up the corporate ladder' and we overall, think about our needs being met before others.

Now, with that being said, we are still good, caring, and loving. And, the more we feel others extending themselves to us, the more we will extend ourselves back to them.

Interesting how that works, isn't it?

If you want to have a strong following of people that admire you, believe in you and respect you, then give yourself emotionally to them first.

After all, how can you expect people to sacrifice their time, energy and money in you when you won't do the same for them? Become interested in what they have to say.

Ask questions about their life. If you're on a date, turn the date on your date— meaning, show how interested you are every facet of their life.

If you're in a work setting where you want to become well-liked and respected, extend yourself with curiosity. Talk to colleagues you've never talked to before about their family, their latest work project.

Become involved in the work culture. Become involved in order to show them your winning spirit (you don't just care about your needs being met, but the needs of everyone around you.)

If that doesn't get you loyal followers, nothing will!

The Prosperity Principle

Who said achieving true wealth and happiness had to be difficult? The truth is, the world is divided into two kinds of people—those that are successful, and those that have stopped trying to be successful (so they never master the skill of what it takes to be successful.)

There are a handful of simple strategies that you can do to leverage your finances and career so that virtually any goal you have will be realized in a very short period of time.

I myself, as well as many of my wealthy friends have applied these techniques.

While some of them may be ideas you've never heard before and outside of your comfort zone, I like to remember this: "The best stuff comes from stepping outside of your comfort zone."

It's true—so instead of thinking about how far you have to go to make your dreams come true (compared to where you are today, right now), take just one step.

Pick just one technique I've laid out for you, and you'll soon be living the life of your dreams. It's not a theory—it's a fact:

Spend one hour a day strengthening a new skill. Some people get really bitter about not having opportunity to advance their career, or for never getting their 'big break.'

But in my experience, you can't get your big break without mentally setting yourself up for it. Let's say you want to become a professional actor, but currently you're an accountant for a corporation firm.

If you're really serious about becoming an actor, you have to start somewhere. You can't even allow the thought of, "How could I EVER become a professional actor," to seep into your consciousness—and you do this by rolling up your sleeves and diving into the work.

Spend just one hour a day learning about something related to acting. Take an acting class once a week. Read books about perfecting your craft and autobiographies written by your favorite actors/actresses. Take it piece by piece, and before long, you'll begin to become mentally and physically the actor you always wanted to be.

Develop micro and macro goals. Goal setting is the key to reaching your prosperity fuelled goals. Just think about it—how can possible become wealthier with a career you absolutely love if you don't believe you can?

The truly successful share many traits, with one of the most powerful being, they success is fuelled by their passion. What are you passionate about?

Once you have answered that, answer this next important question: what realistic goals can I set for myself this week, next week, next month, six months from now and one year from now?

Make sure your goals are attainable, believable and challenge you enough to rise to the occasion.

Then (and here's the real key to success) focus on attaining each goal—not the OUTCOME.

When you focus on the challenge, you forget how far away your ultimate goal is, and enjoy the process—taking pride in your accomplishments along the way. Then, pretty soon, you've arrived at your final destination and can live out the prosperous life you set for yourself.

Wealth is a consequence for your actions. No one owes you wealth—it's simply a consequence for your day to day actions. Many people who want to become wealthy don't understand this, but all the millionaires I know (who are extremely hard working) take pride in the fact that they worked hard to get to where they are, and they don't take it for granted.

Remind yourself that every day that you push yourself, and steadily make progress towards your goals, you will be given the ultimate consequence—true, limitless prosperity.

The *triumph catapult clip*. In order to have a wealthy mindset (and achieve more wealth than you could ever imagine), you need to think how the wealthy think.

The triumph catapult clip technique is all about rising through the ranks in your chosen career so you can get the promotions and raises you crave.

It's about looking for the win/win and leveraging the skills of others in order to give you the outcome you want.

Let's say that you want to become a writer, but after several attempt to finish your novel, you give up.

You just can't figure out an ending that you like, and are bogged down by limiting thoughts such as, "Why do I even bother? I'll never finish this!" Your marketing friend offers to help you, but you decline, feeling like a failure of a writer. The truly successful and wealthy don't feel like this.

They look for the opportunity within each setback and approaches conflict with the *triumph catapult clip*, instead of feeling defeated.

If a millionaire wants to become a novelist, he may take a class on overcoming writer's block, or would seek out his marketing friend to help him learn how to SELL the book (valuable information that could amount to you becoming a best-seller.)

In order to become wealthy, you have to think like the wealthy. Do you have a setback you recently went through?

What opportunity is there for you to learn something, in order to become better, smarter, and wiser?

Who can you partner up to leverage both of your successes to new heights? Make the lesson your focus, not the failure of a project/attempt that didn't work out the way you thought.

Flood your mind with positives. Everyone has thoughts of fear, panic, sadness, boredom and complacency every once in a while. But, the wealthy have learned how to become positive thinking experts.

If you're not getting the outcome you want, you might have a tendency to feel sorry for yourself, or feel like the victim ("Why does this always happen to me?") but the wealthy think differently.

They redirect their attention on the good, the positive and the abundance they do have in their life. To the wealthy, everything is an opportunity for something better to happen.

Anything can happen and because of this mentality, the wealth take risks, continually go outside their comfort zone and become innovators. Flood your mind was positives.

If you have a large amount of negative thoughts coming into your mind every day, that's ok. Simply start by acknowledgement the thought (running away from it will only make it come back with a vengeance later!).

Thank it for showing up, and then redirect your focus on a thought that makes you feel good about yourself. It could be something that you recently accomplished, or it could be a personality trait that you take pride in ("I'm a really amazing cook!").

Focus on the thought for as long as you can, and repeat this exercise any time a negative thought makes its way into your conscious mind.

Pretty soon, you'll find what every wealthy person has—you won't have those pesky, negative thoughts anymore. Think about how liberating that will be!

Mimic your mentor. The truly successful and wealthy know the power behind mentorship.

In fact, many of them probably didn't get to where they are without having someone to teach them the secrets of their own success, or to warn them about mistakes they made.

Find someone to look up to, someone that you admire for their success, talent, or unique skill set.

If you can't contact them personally (let's say they are a celebrity or high profile business person), buy books or attend conferences that they teach.

Many people will organize webinars (totally free) that will allow you to learn valuable information without having to pay anything. Study them, their road to success, and the concepts they apply into their career as though it was your own. Mimic their style, or try out their techniques in your own career—and see where it gets you!

You may be surprised how quickly your financial state can turn around by learning from someone else's.

Know how to leverage a unique skill set (and sell it!) This is one of my favorite techniques, and I fiercely believe that the name of the game (when you want to keep your competitive edge and multiply your wealth, continuously) is by learning and constantly perfecting your unique skill set.

Here's an example: let's say you're a writer, and you've been writing articles and blog posts for clients, for years. But recently, a swarm of younger and cheaper writers have come on the scene—leaving you a bit...disposable.

If you want to get ahead and constantly be at the top of your game, you've got to change your approach to work. Don't keep doing what you've always been doing. Take a look at the most profitable types of writing you can do. Find one that's interests you and study it, practice it, and then continue studying it to make your skill better.

Do you know see how the wealthy thinks? They don't ever fall into a victim trap, or a self- fulfilling prophecy.

They continually build on their own wealth by finding a new outcome, a new growth experience, and a better way to live, to work, and to think. Are you up for the challenge? If so, you're ready to become truly prosperous in every way.

Other External Traits That Make You Likeable

Your body is a billboard for your internal state, but it's not the only advertisement of your intentions and mood. Other factors can actually make a bigger impression over the course of a conversation if you're not careful. Here are some examples:

Your Appearance – How do you look? Are you wearing a ratty old sweatshirt or are you wearing that new pea coat you bought? Comfort is one thing, but sometimes, we feel more comfortable in those ratty old clothes because they make us inconspicuous.

We don't stand out and therefore we don't have to worry about social interactions. Now, if you a leap forward and aim to stand out in what you wear, you'll create a completely different impression. A freshly pressed, squeaky clean appearance can have a huge difference.

Don't get me wrong. The last thing I want anyone reading this to take away is that you need to change to be likable.

Not true – everyone has it in them to be more likable just the way they are, and if you're not comfortable wearing a fancy suit or expensive fragrances, don't worry about it. But, as much as you can look good when you enter these situations.

Psychologists point to social theories like the ones we discussed in the introduction. When you see someone's positive reaction to your clothing and carefully preened exterior, you *feel* more important based on their observations.

Part of it is an illusion, but the confidence gained there allows you to be more proactively engaged with the person you've just met.

Your Voice – How you talk and what you say has nearly as big of an impression on someone you meet as anything else. You should be as inviting as possible, building the impression that you literally have nothing at all you'd rather do than talk to your conversation partner at that moment.

It goes further than just saying "hi" in a convincing tone, though. Your voice needs to show off just how happy you are to talk to someone – be excited and energetic.

If you are happy to see them, show excitement in your voice. If you are unsure of something, make it clear with the inflection you use.

And make sure to speak clearly and consistently. Many shy people have a habit of mumbling their way through a conversation. It's a defence mechanism – if other people cannot hear what you're saying, they cannot judge you for it. However,

it can create an uncomfortable situation for everyone involved and weaken the effect of whatever you're saying, so be clear and commanding in your voice at all times.

Your Attention Span – While not totally related to body language, this is a big one that can totally sink a conversation, even if you're doing everything else right. You must be engaged and interested in everything they have to say for every moment of the conversation, no matter how many distractions there are around you.

Technology is a whopping distraction, so make sure that doesn't become an issue in the future. However, along with technology, you should cut out as many other distractions as possible. If you're trying to meet someone at a bar, keep your friends out of sight and definitely don't check out anyone else while talking to the first person you have on the hook.

If you're at work, put that project aside while you talk with your boss or colleague. You won't get much extra done if you push forward – you'll just come across as rude and obnoxious for not stopping to talk.

The goal here is to maintain your attention span well enough that you can control when the conversation ends. If you really cannot wait any longer for whatever is distracting you, take action and detach from the conversation.

No one will hold it against you if you step back and focus on something else for a few moments, as long as you don't cut off whoever you're talking to or run off without explaining the situation.

How you interact with someone is going to have a major effect on what they think of you. You may like everything they like, be a confident, smooth person, and feel good in your new suit, but if you don't listen, enjoy the conversation and control the way in which your interaction moves forward, it's all for naught.

You'll waste the good will you've built up when they wind up thinking you're rude and uninterested.

Exercises and Questions

1. Have someone follow you around with a video camera or a notebook and record your body language. Review it when you are done to see if you were successful in your changes.

2. Go to a popular social spot and sit in a corner, watching other people interact. See who is successful and what they do that is different from those that fail.

3. Keep a log of the changes you make to your body language and how many people you talk to each night.

4. Record your voice and play it back once a day. You could read the newspaper, talk about your day, or use a phone message. The goal is to become familiar with the tones and inflections of your voice and how they sound to other people.

5. Ask someone how they see you when you meet them. This could be in a bar, at a club, or at work.

Chapter Six:

Humour and Likability

As if it's any surprise, a big part of being likable is being funny. People with a good sense of humour and a clever way with words are generally more popular.

How do you tap the infinite power of humour and put yourself out there as the ultimate likable person? It starts with understanding what other people actually find funny. You'd be shocked how many people think they are funny only to find out that they come across as rude, obnoxious and generally annoying.

Of course, defining humour is kind of conceited – everyone has a different view on what is funny and how to tap into that powerful torrent of laugh lines and clever insights.

So, I won't get scientific on you here; rather let's just focus on what I've done and have seen work in the past, and how you can start generating a personality that other people find endearing and funny.

What's Funny?

"No one ever looked stupid when they were having fun." – Unknown So, what's funny?

Everyone wants to laugh—so, the more humor you bring into your life, the better ability you'll have to bring the masses to you!

Here are some tips to help you get started:

Don't Take Anything too Seriously – The easiest way to ruin a humorous conversation is to take any single thing too seriously. Stay loose, don't get upset by anything unless you're sure someone is trying to poke at you, and just generally stay relaxed.

Avoid Sombre Topics – Some topics just aren't funny. Stay away from the story of how your cat got hit by a car in high school or how your little brother has the Measles. It just doesn't work when you're trying to be funny. On the flip side, it's possible to take some topics that are otherwise sombre and make them funny. For example, I was in a bar once and found out my wallet had been stolen between the cab and the bar.

I was very upset, but rather than letting it ruin my evening, I made a couple of jokes about the thief getting a free sandwich from Quizno's for his trouble.

It broke the tension, helped me and my friends relax and allowed me to continue enjoying the night (once I'd called in my stolen credit cards and ID).

Make Casual Observations Interesting – If you see someone walk into a room with a barber pole striped cane or a child wearing a giant pair of sunglasses, you have free material. Remember not to make fun of anyone and don't make comments about stereotypes or prejudices, but common observations about other people in a fun loving way can be hilarious when done properly.

Jokes Are Good – Energy is Better – A formal joke can be funny, but really it's about the delivery. Just reciting a joke doesn't always work. I'm sure you've had a friend try to remember a joke and completely kill its delivery, leading to polite laughter from one and all. If you can maintain an energetic attitude and build on whatever you feel about a certain joke, I guarantee the actual content matters far less than how you deliver it.

Reference Past Jokes for Greater Impact – Inside jokes are a great way to build rapport. You can create in-jokes easily by referencing a joke you made earlier in a conversation. Here's another example from one of my nights out. A friend showed up wearing this hilariously garish purple leopard striped t-shirt. My comment: "Look guys, Barney mated with a snow leopard." Nothing too deep there – an easy joke. But, later that night, when my buddy got turned down by a woman he was falling over himself to meet, I made a joke about Barney getting free hugs and cheered him right up.

Cultural Jokes and Pop Culture References – An easy way to be funny is with cultural jokes and pop culture references. Most people are at least partially caught up on the latest celebrity gossip, TV show references, or movie trivia. If you make a joke about Brad and Angelina, most people will get the reference. These jokes are tricky – you need to know your audience and create something interesting and funny (not just rehashing Tonight Show jokes). Everyone has a different sense of humour and unfortunately they don't carry plaques attached to their heads that says "I'm sarcastic" or "I'm a little dry". So, you'll need to feel them out a bit when you first start talking. This will take some practice to get the hang of, but you'll quickly learn to make the most of the material you've developed.

Funny Examples

Now you know what types of things work as humour, but what about the actual content of what you say? What can you talk about that will lead to chuckles and head nods from the people you meet? Here are a few of my favourite funny options for this kind of situation.

Unexpected Actions

When something happens that no one expects, people tend to laugh. This is a common theme in British humour - Monty Python, for example.

Just watch as John Cleese and his buddies go from throwing fish around to fighting over the weight of a coconut in one of their films or television specials.

Half of what happens makes no sense and nothing can be predicted. I won't ruin it for anyone who hasn't already seen it to say that the ending of Monty Python and Holy Grail fits the bill perfectly – it's out of left field and therefore it's hilarious.

So how do you tap the unexpected to be entertaining to your new friends or a potential boyfriend? You can make the unexpected happen, or you can simply make observations about things that happen that no one expects.

Reality seems pretty dull at times, but you'd be surprised how often something happens without any context or warning that could be a perfectly funny joke. A man wearing a tutu, a dog running on his hind legs, a two year old with wraparound sunglasses – they're silly, strange, and if you have a good quip ready, very funny.

Overreacting

Playful overreaction is hilarious if done properly. Making jokes about how long something takes or how big something is and blowing it out of proportion is good material if delivered in a playful tone. It also works for less direct things.

Just take a look at a comic strip and look for easy, overreaction jokes in images. They only have three panels to work with, so it makes sense that they could go over the top with a couple strokes of the pen and it would be funny.

For example, Garfield eats an unhealthy, generally impossible amount of food – often times in the form of cheesy goodness that should have killed him 20 years ago. That cat is like 32 years old and he just keeps eating. How the heck is that possible? I don't know, but a lot of people over the years have found it quite funny (note: not everyone thinks Garfield is funny).

Wordplay

The most common type of wordplay is sexual innuendo (at least the most common if you're in a bar or are a teenager). Taking something said by someone out of context and using it sexually will almost always get a big laugh.

A note about this type of humour - it can quickly get you in trouble with people if you're not careful. Making sexual jokes to a male co-worker, for example, can get you fired (or at the very least stuck in a two day seminar discussing why you made said joke). Watch the word play if you're unsure of what the words mean. You'll embarrass yourself.

When it comes time to tell a joke, share a funny thought or otherwise engage people with your charming, sophisticated self, you'd better be ready for it. Remember how bad that joke was when told by someone who wasn't ready for it? Awful – simply awful.

So, we're going to churn things up a notch and kick them out at a different pace, using careful approaches to humour that actually work.

Being Goofy

Walk down the street and point out anyone you think is funny. The guy wearing the suit, with a pale complexion, pleated pants and brand new briefcase? Not funny. The guy wearing the checked pants, big hat, and bright red nose?

Hilarious (and also a clown). The goofier you are and the goofier you act, the funnier you will be.

It's the same reason people will laugh at a horrible movie when at a movie theatre. They are in a theatre, with other people laughing and therefore they feel that they are supposed to laugh. Their brain plays a cruel trick on their eyes and convinces them that what they are seeing is funny.

I'm not saying that someone laughing at your joke is simply the victim of cruelty inflicted upon them by their subconscious (for your sake, I hope not), but if you play the part, they're a heck of a lot more likely to laugh when you say something funny.

How do you act goofy? Pretty much just relax and sink into the role of the funny guy in the group. Remember the class clown from school? He pretty much said whatever was on his mind and did things that were borderline against the rules. Follow his lead – people will find it hilarious.

Practice Your Delivery

Humour is based almost entirely on how you say something. Again, if two guys told a cheap knock-knock joke, the guy with the effective delivery would pull it off and the guy with that tight tie and new briefcase would get some polite chuckles.

Sitting in front of a mirror and telling jokes is probably not the best way to go about practicing your funny bone, but it definitely doesn't hurt. I recommend you get out there and spend some time with people who will find you funny.

Friends, family, loved ones – they will boost your ego with easy laughs and let you relax a bit. The more relaxed you are, the more naturally these funny jokes come to mind and the easier it is to be funny.

In the end, humour comes from practice. It's like a contact sport, but with laughter and frowns instead of broken ribs and touchdowns. Practice enough and you'll get more of one than the other.

Tell it Smoothly

Remember your public voice. Tell things clearly, be careful in how you setup, describe and deliver your jokes and maintain a steady voice as you tell them.

People are much more likely to not only listen to you but find your thoughts and observations funny if you say them with conviction and confidence than if you stumble over your delivery in a quiet, easily misunderstood murmur. Oh, and if you have to repeat anything, it's not funny.

Chapter Seven:

Communication

Communication is the core of all relationships. If you can't talk to someone, you won't be getting anywhere as their friend or girlfriend.

So, I've devoted this chapter to helping you understand what people expect to hear, how to say it, and more importantly, how to develop rapport through what you say.

There's a lot to basic communication that can impact your social life – keep reading for more details on how to take advantage of it rather than be terrified by it.

Forget What Other People Think

We've already touched on this one a little bit – other people *don't* actually spend a whole lot of time thinking about you.

Most of them are equally as worried about your impression of them. So when you meet someone for the first time, the last thing on your mind should be "what do they think" or "what will they say".

The truth is, they're just as concerned about what you think of them as you are.

Wiping Away the Memories of Failure

When I flash back to third grade, the only things I can immediately remember are the embarrassing moments I had – the time I got sick in the middle of the playground, the time I wasn't allowed on a field trip because my dog peed on the permission slip, and the time I lost my shorts in the pool during swim lessons. I have to dig around a little bit to find the good memories.

They are there, but they tend to get buried down by the stuff that is embarrassing – you know, the memories you'd rather didn't exist. After so many years, those memories are less embarrassing and more hilarious than anything, but for a long time, they were the lowlights of the year.

Our brains have a nasty habit of looking for whatever was least likable about a situation and then smothering us with it in a new situation.

So, when we meet a new person, we don't think "wow, someone I can get to know"; we think of how we accidentally had toilet paper on our shoe or had a goofy looking hairstyle the last time we were on a date.

Step one to improving your communication skills is cutting these unwanted memories out and focusing on the 'here and now'.

Your brain may want to focus on everything bad that ever happened to you on a date, but when you're on a date, every ounce of your attention needs to be in the here and now. Not the past. Not the future. The immediate moment.

Here's how to do just that:

Anytime you're feeling concerned, worried or insecure, remember this one little thing.

The one little thing I'm referring to is how much the other person is worried, or insecure too.

Be on the same team!

You can actually eradicate feelings of fear by connecting with the other person on an emotionally level. "Whew. You seem really normal! I promise you I am too.

Plus, you know, the first two minutes of a date are the scariest, and we've gotten through that, so let's see what else we can get through."

Then, smile. Congratulations!

You've just put your date at ease, and communicated that you're human. You're real. You're authentic.

And, chances are you're someone that your date REALLY wants to get to know now.

Draw on Confidence to Be Sure of Self

Self-assurance is a strange thing, mostly in that it's incredibly hard to attain and hold on to. When you set foot in public, the first thing you do is wonder what other people will think.

Why? Is it because you're worried what they think or because you want validation of your actions? What pushes you to worry so much about what other people have to say about you?

Finding the strength to stand up for yourself and essentially say "I am important and what other people think of my opinions is not important" is hard.

However, affirmations make it a lot easier!

Here are some confidence boosting thoughts of intention that will allow you to begin believing in the very thing you want to achieve:

- "I'm enough, just as I am, right now."
- "I'm intelligent, otherwise I wouldn't be here."

- "I'm positive, and focused on the good in life, which allows people to gravitate   towards me."
- "People see me, and how trustworthy I am."
- "I breathe in security, and self-assurance, and I breath out fear, and self-doubt."
- "My life is full of passion and electric energy, which attracts others to me, every   single day."

You'll need to practice, and eventually there will be tests for your new attitude, especially when you come across people you respect and want to know more closely.

For now, think of it this way – you are the center of attention at all times. Other people are guests in your reality and they need to act accordingly, which means if anyone should be worried about how they are perceived, it is them.

The effect will be that you feel surer of yourself and that other people will feed off that confidence and show interest in what you have to say more readily.

How to Listen to Other People

Before we go any further I want to make it very clear what I mean by "communication".

 It's not just talking to someone, or even clarifying a point. Really, it's 90% listening and maybe 10% talking. If you're not a good listener, you're not a good communicator – pure and simple. But, it goes beyond that.

We hear cliché jokes and insults all the time about people who "just don't listen". That's not really what I mean, though it can definitely be a problem for a lot of individuals trying to engage with a new friend or romantic interest.

124

In your case, what's happening is slightly different. You're uncomfortable around people, unsure of yourself and generally very self-conscious. So, what happens? You get worked up and start running through a million scenarios, reminders to "stop doing X" and constant negative self-talk.

Have you ever tried to remember what someone was saying to you when that tempest of anxiety whirls through your brain?

It's pretty freaking hard. And as a result, it's impossible to feel engaged (or look engaged) to someone you might actually be interested in getting to know.

I had a problem for years where I would never remember anyone's name when I met them. I couldn't figure out why, but it would constantly put me into uncomfortable situations trying to jog my memory or sneaking aside to whisper to someone "what's the guy's name again".

Eventually, I figured out what I was doing. I was so worked up and focused on worrying about the conversation I was *about to have* that I missed the beginning of that conversation, instantly making it WAY more complicated than it needed to be.

So, I started consciously clearing my mind when I met someone, using mnemonic devices to memorize their name immediately and focusing all of my energies into listening to what they were saying.

It was incredibly hard at first, but in time, I learned that I was pretty dang good at listening to people...if I stopped worrying about the little things that would so easily distract me.

Fast forward a few years and I'm in a completely different place in my relationships. I don't just memorize people's names; I file away tons of little details about them for later use.

People are impressed with my steel-trap memory, but really most of us have the same ability – we just need to clear out the white noise and focus on what people are saying.

Clearing Out the White Noise

The first step in effectively listening to someone is to clear out the white noise that takes up your brain's active space during a conversation. It's not easy – in fact, it's one of the hardest things you'll do when talking to someone.

Because, let's face it, 90% of the problems you have in conversation are directly related to not feeling comfortable. Those thoughts are the direct reason for that discomfort and making them stop is a process.

This chapter is loaded with information on how to build rapport and convince people to let you into their little world in the form of a conversation, but eventually you must learn how to invite them into your world, which honestly can be much harder, especially if you're uncomfortable sharing those details about yourself.

This is where your internal voice goes to town, psyching you out about what it's okay to say, what it's not okay to say, and what the other person will think about all of it.

I could tell you to relax and be yourself, but there are boundaries that need to be adhered to. Forget those boundaries and it's easy to scare other people away.

Give Enough Away to Build Interest

Here's what happens. You feel uncomfortable sharing any information about yourself, so you pull back, lock it all up, and don't say a word, even though your conversation partner is interested in learning more.

For example, I've worked with many people who are hopelessly unable to network with their colleagues at events designed for networking. They go into the conversation not wanting to talk about themselves, feeling embarrassed that they may be bragging or going on at too much length about what they do.

It's a bad habit, because a lot of people do want to know what you do - at least to some degree.

They need to have an impression of you as a whole if they are going to contact you in the future for work related needs. Exchanging this kind of information is how the business world works and if you're out looking for a date or a friend, it's even more relevant to the conversation.

You need to be willing to give away bits and pieces of yourself in conversation so that you can build an impression upon your conversational partner and they can understand your motivations and interests more readily.

Here are just a few fun things you can give away early in a conversation to build rapport and keep the back and forth alive.

Opinions on Major Events or Ideas – If you're talking about a recent news event or an idea or concept that you have an opinion on, share your opinion. Don't be overbearing with your opinion (always be open to hear someone else out), but by sharing your own thoughts, you give away a bit of yourself to open up a relationship with that new person. They will see that sharing as an invitation to return it in kind.

Your Name and Occupation – The simplest way to start any conversation is by telling someone who you are, and not just "Hi my name is Barry". You need to say your full name, what you do if it comes up and why you are in whatever location you are in.

A Hobby or Activity You Enjoy – Bringing up activities or hobbies you enjoy will personalize you even more so than simply outlining an opinion. Mention a recent outing, describe what you do in your spare time, or talk about something you just learned related to your hobby.

Your Spouse or Children – Mentioning your family can be a big way to build rapport and show that you are comfortable in a conversation. Do it casually and only if it's called for. Some people grow uncomfortable at the constant mention of children or spouses, so don't overdo it – just make casual mention so they feel more comfortable in your presence.

Your Current Goal – Why are you talking to this person? If you're networking, make it clear what your business goals are. If you're looking for a date, feel free to admit it. Early honesty backed up with interesting conversation will endear you to many people quickly.

The key to giving information away is to do it subtly. Here's what I mean by that:

John: *Hi, my name is John – I've been here for a few hours, looking for someone in the HVAC industry who might be interested in our products.*

Sue: *Nice to meet you John. I'm Sue – not in HVAC, unfortunately, but I did run into a couple guys back at the bar 10 minutes ago or so.*

John: *Maybe you can help me hunt them down in a few minutes. For now, let's just say I'm on a break (just between you and me). Billy can take care of things for now.*

Sue: *Haha, sure thing. I'm just about ready for another drink anyways. Billy's your partner?*

John: *Yeah, he's all over this networking stuff. We call him our Sales Ninja – in a dozen places at once.*

I could go on, but you get the gist.

John didn't have to say "my sales partner, Billy". He just said "Billy" and created an opening for Sue to ask about him. It's a trick that works with any piece of information and in nearly any situation. By acting like you already know this person – like they should already know who Billy is – you generate instant rapport with them.

In this case, Sue is already comfortable with John after two exchanges and hints at getting a drink with him. He even kicks it up a notch by making a joking reference to her being in on his unsolicited break.

The information you give away can be nearly anything, but the more smoothly you give it away, the better the effect will be.

Here are some examples of what NOT to do when trying to share:

Lies or Stretches of the Truth – If you try to make yourself look so attractive to someone that they cannot possibly resist, you risk a major issue when they start either questioning the believability of your claims or they actually fall for it and you're forced to either admit your lies or continue with them until the end of the relationship (which usually coincides with admitting your lies). You've seen it in a million sitcoms – don't let your life sprout a laugh track.

Trying to Get 100% Approval – No one in the world, no matter how likable they are, is liked by everyone. Everyone has a different outlook on life and it will inevitably clash with someone else, so don't go in trying to project your "perfect self" in hopes of impressing the people you meet. It rarely works.

Vague Statements – If you're truthful but you have a nasty habit of being entirely too vague about what you say, the odds are that you'll fail in the process because people won't believe you. Make clear, specific statements. Don't say "I taught middle school." Instead go with "I taught at Alderwood Middle School until 2003". The human brain will assume truthfulness if you fill in all the holes as you tell your story. Leave them blank and it will ask "why didn't he say where or when?"

Own Your Statements – A lot of people are afraid to take responsibility and ownership of their statements. So they defer ownership by using rhetorical situations or using pronouns like "we" or "you". My theory is that if you really are not sure of an opinion, you probably shouldn't share it. If you believe something and want other people to know it, you should just say "I believe this..." It's more responsible and makes you instantly more likable. Someone could completely disagree with you, but will respect and like your conviction.

Holding Your Cards too Close – I had a problem for a long time in which I would gloss over details about my life that I thought were dull to other people. To me, what I did for a living wasn't that interesting or they had preconceptions that I was projecting onto them. In truth, most people are very interested in what I do, but I never gave them the opportunity to learn more because I covered it all up.

There are quite a few things that can mess up a conversation; if you follow common sense and are truthful and open about yourself and what you hope to get out of the exchange, though, I think you'll find that all that stress goes right out the window.

Back to Listening

This all brings us back to the act of listening – that simple yet for some reason overwhelming activity that will act as the foundation of all good conversation. Here's where things get simple (seriously!)

Push away all of the thoughts that have been bugging you about the conversation. Pretend the person you're talking to hasn't had a single thought about you – this is a blank slate on which you can draw whatever picture you want.

Now, honestly listen to what they have to say.

A major problem many people have in conversation is getting lost on a topic. People will discuss the weather, the wellbeing of their families, their pets, local sports and recent news and then run out of topics. The well dries up and both people grow uncomfortable.

Why does this happen? Because you aren't really listening to what the other person has to say.

You'll be shocked by just how much information comes up in the course of regular conversation. People say things all the time that get left by the wayside. You have a thought in mind and want to say it, and therefore ignore whatever the other person has to say, plowing through and then ending the conversation as quickly as it started.

Next time you feel uncomfortable in a conversation, try this instead: pay close attention to everything someone has to say. Now, instead of telling anecdotes about yourself or changing the topic to something you've had on your mind, ask questions or make comments about your partner's commentary.

The idea is simple – you focus heavily on the input you're receiving and use that to frame everything you have to say. If you don't, you'll completely run out of things to say and of course become uncomfortable. With time, this technique will help you generate a much greater appreciation for the input you receive in a conversation.

Caveat to Listening

Of course, there are certain circumstances where you're expected to take the lead in a conversation – notably in dating. No one is comfortable when meeting someone for the first time. Therefore, when you first meet someone, you should be willing to build on the conversation from any point at any time.

It's not easy, but the ability to change the subject rapidly at any time will help you develop a powerful rapport with them and create a conversational strain that pretty much cannot die. Not easy, but well worth the effort.

Active Listening

In his book "Conversationally Speaking" Alan Garner describes Active Listening as how you interpret what someone is saying and repeat it back to them so that you can make sure it is accurate.

Why is this important? Because so many of us are terrified of getting it wrong. And worse yet, many people don't even consider that they may have heard someone incorrectly in the first place.

What happens is that someone says something, it gets taken out of context and the entire conversation (and possibly the relationship) gets turned on its head because of a misunderstanding.

Differences in sense of humor, conversational style, and general beliefs can all create this problem, so it's very important to clarify what's being said before you respond.

Here's an example: Jennifer: *I can't believe they gave you that promotion.*

John could respond in one of two ways initially – either in indignation if he thinks she is angry at him for taking the promotion or with sympathy if he feels she is upset that it wasn't her. It might even be a joke. So, to be sure that he has taken it the right way, John should say something like:

John: *You're frustrated that you're still in the same position?*

John asks instead of assuming, giving Jennifer the opening needed to clarify. It keeps the conversation moving, avoids awkward misunderstandings and generates rapport because John appears concerned about Jennifer's plight, while deferring the conversation from his own good fortune.

John listened to her problem, interpreted it in a certain way and then, through active listening, asked for clarification on what he perceived – the idea being that if he's wrong, she'll say so without getting angry. It works almost every time.

Use this technique whenever you're unsure of what someone means or if the statement feels like it could be easily mistaken.

Emotionally charged, seemingly angry or upset statements should always be parsed in this way. It helps you to gather your response to it, but it also ensures you don't take anything the wrong way and create an unnecessary uncomfortable situation.

Verbal Cues in a Conversation

In "How to Make People Like You in 90 Seconds" Nicholas Boothman discusses his perception of human sensory preferences. He describes three types of people – Auditory, Visual, and Kinaesthetic. Basically, different people prefer different types of interaction and will interact with others based on that style. They will describe things based on how they saw, heard, or felt it, and if you can easily pick up on that preference, you'll have a much easier time engaging in conversation with them.

So, what we're trying to do is to pick up on as quickly as possible what these types of people prefer in their conversational style. Then, we can flip it around and provide a more specialized conversation that they can engage in. After all, imagine how someone who is an auditory talker would respond if you didn't clarify any points and used a lot of wild hand gestures. They'd likely get lost and therefore relatively bored, effectively ending your conversation before it really got off the ground.

Auditory Verbal Cues – Auditory cues include any words that relate hearing or understanding through an audio interaction. Anything that describes speech or the interaction of speech, like *discuss, talk, hear, remark, describe*, etc. falls into this category.

Visual Verbal Cues – Visual cues include any words that relate to sight, either directly or metaphorically. For example, someone might say "I see" a lot and to them, it is as if they can literally see the truth behind what you're saying. They could just as easily say "I understand" or "I hear you", but they don't – instead utilizing a strong visual cue. Look for other visual cues in their speech like colours, shades, and active looking phrases.

Kinaesthetic Verbal Cues - Some people cannot interact through audio or visual cues. They need to hold the conversation in their hands and feel how it develops. For you, that means to look for phrases like *feel* or *grasp* instead of "understand". Look for other active, physical words as well, especially when used to describe something. These types of talkers will often describe something kinaesthetically even without having touched it. For example, they might say "the road was rough" instead of "the road made the car rattle".

The idea behind this exercise, as Boothman outlines in his book is that by better understanding what someone looks for in a conversation, you can cater your responses to the sensory reception that best suits them. But, it goes beyond that. You won't just say things in the way they best understand them, you can provide specific cues that fit their personality.

For example, a visual talker will get a lot of conversational value out of hand gestures, while an audio talker needs specific details of a story and a kinaesthetic talker will want to hold and touch the details. This knowledge can also come in handy in a dating scenario. If someone is a kinaesthetic conversationalist, you'll know early on that touching will be a part of a standard conversation and not a misinterpreted signal.

Developing Rapport

"In the end these things matter most: how well did you love? How fully did you live? How deeply did you let go?" — Gautama Buddha

When it comes to meeting someone and starting a conversation, the "R" word is one of the most fundamental aspects of the process.

Without rapport, you'll never be able to create a connection with someone you just met. With too much forced rapport, you come across as a bit needy.

The key is to tap into the natural rapport any two adult human beings have with each other, and then pinpoint key similarities and interests that will allow you to generate additional rapport and create a closer connection.

Sounds complicated, but we've already gone over a number of tips that will help you tap those connections that you may not even realize exist.

The 10 Things You Instantly Communicate When You Meet Someone

If you and I met tomorrow I'd be able to immediately determine 10 things about you as a person, based solely on the combination of body language, introductions, and general attitude you display.

These early indicators can sink a conversation off the bat, or they can act as a tool you can use to build rapport instantly with the people you meet. Here's how:

Intelligence – Intelligence comes across in the first few words you say. The problem with this one is that the initial impression you make doesn't necessarily reflect your actual intelligence. That's why having something smart and interesting to talk about is so important.

Confidence – How you stand, the timber of your voice, the eye contact you make, and the decisions you select will show just how confident you are.

Intentions – Your intentions in the conversation will blaze out of you in the conversation. This is especially true in dating situations where you are trying to convey a sense of sexual interest – your body will scream interest.

Mindset – Your current mind set is an open book. If you're uncomfortable, distracted or simply not paying attention, they'll know immediately. So, get in a good mind set before you engage.

Interest – Your interest in them is also very evident by the questions you ask and how observant you are. Carefully analyzing them, developing a clear idea of what you want and then sharing that will showcase your interest almost instantly.

Sense of Humor – Be funny right away because it's vital to establish that sense of humor early.

Adaptability – If something happens, as is often the case in a crowded environment, how do you react? If you're really interested in someone, a distraction from the bar or a friend shouldn't stop your advances.

Communicativeness – Your ability to articulate and communicate a thought are not only displayed immediately, they are used to inform other things on this list such as intelligence and mind set.

Focus – Your focus is completely unrelated to your mind set in that it defines how clearly defined your goals are. If you're watching other people, they know your goal is to mingle, not to create relationships. Be clear about your goal both internally and externally.

Clarity – Clarity of statements and actions defines just how sure of yourself you are. The less clear you are, the less sure you seem.

Rapport is a powerful tool that salesmen, pickup artists, and politicians alike harness and generate out of thin air.

You may not become the next great meet and greeter, but you can tap into what people are feeling and make the most out of a meeting with little more than the basic tools I'm about to show you.

Natural Rapport

While many books will talk about developing rapport and creating a connection with someone you just met (especially the dating guru guides), most of them skip something very important – the idea of natural rapport.

Believe it or not, every single person has some degree of connection with every other individual on the planet.

You could meet someone for the first time and feel at least some connection with them. You are both humans, have undergone the same growth and development cycles and are bound to understand at least a handful of things the same way.

Truly likable people are those who can determine where that natural rapport lies and tap into it immediately, building on it with as many interactions as possible.

It's like having radar that tells you what the person you've just met thinks of you and what they desire in someone they've just met.

Chance Rapport

Natural rapport is powerful and if you tap into it effectively, it can develop into a long term connection with any random stranger you happen to run into.

But, there is another kind of rapport that seemingly comes out of thin air – chance rapport.

This is when you run into someone who just so happens to have the same interests, beliefs, values, or ideas as you.

It doesn't happen very often and if you were out looking for a romantic interest, you'd likely think you'd just met your soul mate, but it does happen and you should be ready to take advantage of it when it does.

Changing the Rapport You Develop

Now, for the most important part of the equation – changing the rapport you happen to develop once it has been generated.

Meeting someone, finding out you both love the same movies and music and that you are both equally inept storytellers doesn't mean you will get along with one another infinitely. You still need to generate the rapport that leads to friendship (or something more).

How to Treat Someone You've Just Met – When you first meet someone, the conversation will be based on nothing more than the casual interest you generate in those first few seconds. If you cannot do that, people will grow bored and walk away. Remember, they're going to ask "what's in this for me" and it's your job to show them as quickly as possible. So, when you meet, you should treat them like old friends – buddies that can rely on each other and that will help one another when they need it. Think on how you'd greet an old college or high school friend and act the same with anyone you meet for the first time. That rapport immediately generates feelings that you're a valuable person to know.

Building a Relationship out of Nothing – From here, you can start creating a new relationship pretty much out of thin air. Start leaking bits and pieces about who you are and what you have to offer the interaction and people will quickly warm to you and your personality.

How to Talk About Shared Interests – Shared interests are the key to developing further rapport, but I should caution you before you start trying to show off all the things you *also* like to do. If you claim too main shared interests, it often comes across the wrong way, as someone trying too hard. They will think you're at worst lying and at best trying too hard. Look for honest, real world interests the two of you can share and you'll see what I mean when the conversation goes to the next level.

> Rapport is so powerful that, when not properly handled, it can just as easily backfire and ruin a new relationship as fast as it was created. Don't let that happen – build up from what you have and go from there.

Synchronizing with Other People

If you've read anything else about body language, meeting people, or generating rapport, you've probably heard about synchronizing. For the most part, I don't recommend this for dating or picking up the opposite sex.

There is a very fine power structure between a man and a woman when they first meet. You might be more likable by mirroring the other person, but you also tell them that you're not comfortable being yourself and therefore you give away a lot of your own power.

But, this is a book about being likable and posture mirroring and synchronization work wonders when you're trying to become more likable – so much so that I cannot ignore it.

What is this powerful tool that can revolutionize how you interact with people you meet? It's exactly like it sounds – you meet someone and work to mirror their actions in your own.

Very important note here: don't play Simon Says with your new friend. Copying someone too overtly is not only obnoxious; it doesn't reveal anything about you as a person. It simply shows that you're incapable of being interesting on your own terms.

If you can synchronize certain aspects of your interaction with the person you've just met, however, they will feel instantly at ease talking to you. After all, who are you most comfortable with in the world? Yourself, right?

So, if you can offer that to a stranger, they'll fall into an immediately comfortable state that opens them up to you and your conversation.

Posture Mirroring

Everything we've been talking about leads up to a single point – you being able to look at someone, analyze their body language and determine what their mind set is.

When you learn how to do this, you can start posture mirroring. The reason this is such a tricky action is that you really don't want to come across as making fun of them.

Imagine what happens if you stand there copying their every gesture. They might not realize at first, but as time goes by, it will grow awkward and eventually they'll either be offended or weirded out. So, instead of simply mimicking them like a monkey trying to get a banana out of the machine, you should look for the drive *behind* their actions and take on that persona.

If someone is relaxing, leaning back and talking smoothly and calmly, they are relaxed and inviting. Mirror this by relaxing your arms, settling into your chair and slowing the pace of conversation.

If they are excited and energetic, showing it with rapid hand gestures and quick speech, don't necessarily copy their hand gestures, but display your own level of excitement to mirror that attitude.

> In mirroring someone's actions, you create a strong Affinity and Empathy with that person, connecting with them on a level that cannot be reached through conversation alone.

It's all subconscious, but it can lead to a much greater conversation almost immediately.

Again, avoid direct mirroring and if someone is displaying posture and body language indicating discomfort or annoyance, *don't* mirror that. Try to draw them in with your own relaxing body language instead.

Chapter Eight:

Starting Conversations

"What lies behind us and what lies before us are tiny matters compared to what lies withinus."

– Ralph Waldo Emmerson

Right now your mind may be churning. You're worried about what someone would say to you or think about you when you talk to them. You're concerned that you'll get it all wrong; that everything you do or say is a sure way to ruin your future relationship with this person forever.

The point is that conversation is a powerful tool – one that can determine the future course of your life, but when you think of it like that, you just psych yourself out and, let's face it, probably freak out whoever you're talking to.

Finding People Who Want to Talk to You

Let's pretend you're in a situation where you need to talk to strangers. It might be at a bar where you hope to get or give a phone number or it could be a work outing where you should be networking with potential business contacts. It doesn't really matter where it is – the point is that you need to walk up to a stranger, introduce yourself, and then engage in an enjoyable, genial conversation.

Take a deep breath, because this doesn't have to be as hard as it sounds. I have a few tricks up my sleeve. First, let's narrow down our

141

prospects and make sure you only talk to people likely to respond to you positively:

Body Language – People will display certain behaviors if they're interested in talking. Look for uncrossed arms, open legs, upright posture, and someone standing away from the wall, near a crowd. People who are uncomfortable or just plain uninterested will try to make themselves look as unassuming as possible in a corner and fold up into themselves.

Eye Contact – If you're scanning the room and someone avoids eye contact with you, they likely don't want to chat. That may or may not dissuade you, but if you're looking for a willing partner, find someone who returns your gaze and smiles. It's friendly and inviting.

Look for Romantic Cues – If you're trying to meet a guy, look for sexual cues. Men will scan your body quickly, stand straighter, turn their head to the side, but not out of eye contact range, and smile continuously. It's a ritual – once you recognize it, the process gets much easier.

Gauge their Sociability – If someone is talking to five or six other people, and you're still working on developing your conversational skills, I don't recommend you jump into an active conversation. However, if you see them talking genially to different people and they are currently unoccupied, take the opportunity to introduce yourself.

I should crib all of this by saying not to overthink the beginning of a conversation. The last thing you want to do is spend so much time trying to find the "perfect" person to talk to that you end up sitting in the corner smiling and staring at people – you'll become the creepy person that no one wants to talk to. Make a quick decision and get in there. The sooner the better.

Opening a Conversation

The beginning of a conversation is not important. It really isn't, believe it or not. People won't judge you for asking about the weather (unless you fail to think of anything more interesting soon thereafter), nor will they think you are a poet if you have something especially deep and meaningful to say.

The best opener for a conversation is something simple and clichéd like "how are you doing" or "my name is X, it's nice to meet you." Yes, it's simple and no it doesn't give you anything to build off of, but it does create an initial impression, opens the possibility of conversation and gives you an in.

With all that in mind, there are some things you should *never* say when you start a conversation:

Insults or Complaints – Opening with a negative statement about someone or something sets you up as a malcontent and can generally ruin the mood for conversation. It also messes up the other person's initial perception of a smiling, interesting looking person that they saw across the room – just plain not good.

Assumptions – Don't walk up to someone and start making assumptions about who they are or what they believe. It's rude and can make someone very defensive – not a good mood for a conversation with a new person. Be open-minded and if you think you know something, ask a question to confirm – don't make assumptions.

Sexual Overtones – Some highly social people can pull this off if they are subsequently funny and interesting, but for the most part, never open a conversation with a sexually charged statement. This is someone you just met who doesn't know anything about you and your sense of humor. Unless you are very clearly joking and you have reason to believe that they will find it humorous, keep it chaste until a rapport has developed.

Sharing too Much – Opening up so people can get to know you a bit better is an important first step, but it can also go too far and weird people out if they don't know you. Imagine if someone walked up to you in a bar and said "I just had an endoscopy today and my throat is a little raw". No one needs to hear about your personal health issues, dating problems, or family issues. Keep things like this under wraps unless it fits the conversation and helps you develop rapport.

The beginning of a conversation needs to be as simple and straightforward as possible. Trying too hard or being openly rude can severely hurt your chances of effectively opening and carrying on a conversation.

Find Common Ground

The easiest way to open any conversation is to find common ground and elaborate on it. It's why so many people go straight to the weather or current events – it's a shared experience. Everyone has an opinion on the weather or a recent park opening in your city. But, these examples alone don't work as well when you want to learn more about someone. You need something else to switch to quickly if you want to keep a conversation going in a natural way. One tool that can help immensely is humor, which we've already discussed quite a bit. If you're a funny person, people won't care what you talk about. Your observations will be amusing enough to keep them engaged in the conversation until the end. Still, I recommend you find something more immediate and accessible to discuss than the weather or the news.

If you're in a bar, you can talk about the music being played or the ball game on TV. If you're in a work conference, you can discuss the most recent speaker or the quality of the food they're feeding you. These are shared experiences and can often open up further interests on both sides.

Conversational Scenarios

Conversation is like a football game.

There are dozens of potential plays and any one of them can break down at any moment. The best way to prepare for what will happen is to know as many of the plays as possible and watch tape of your opponents.

The better prepared you are, the more seamlessly you can react to what happens. In our case, that means going through potential scenarios in conversation.

Criticism

When someone offers criticism there are a ton of ways to respond. The easiest way is to take it in stride and move on. However, in some cases, you may decide you need more details or specifically that you would like to get tips on how to improve yourself in the future. Here's an example of how this can work:

Bill: Jim, I think you were a little rude to that woman back at the bar.

Jim: How was I rude?

If Jim asks in a polite way without taking it personally and getting defensive, this question can lead to an honestly helpful, eye opening situation where he learns more about how he talks to women. Another thing Jim could say is:

Jim: Can you be more specific?

In this case, Jim asks for more details to generate detail that he can use in the future. Instead of responding with *"what?"* he just asks how he can make a change and goes with it. The final way I like to respond to criticism is with agreement:

Jim: You're right. I don't know what came over me. I just got all worked up. What do you think I should have said?

Here, Jim not only takes the criticism, he admits it is correct and asks for help in correcting the problem.

Criticism in general can be handled in a lot of different ways – how you use it will depend largely on the situation and your usual response to these types of things, but remember, more often than not, criticism is a gift, not something to be upset about.

When Someone Asks You for Something

Often, in a conversation, someone will ask you for something. It might be a piece of information, a favor, or something else that will require you to actively engage them and offer something beyond a simple response.

I like to play this one in one of a couple ways. First, you shouldn't just give someone everything they ask of you. It creates a situation where you can be easily manipulated. However, you want to remain nice and likable so you need to be able to give it to them in the end, just through a trade of information.

Anne: Nice to meet you Joe. What brings you to a place like this?

Joe: Needed to get a bit of air, plus I wanted to see what the full moon brought out this month.

Joe doesn't really answer the question, but provides enough information to keep Anne happy and move forward with the conversation. Here's what would happen if Anne wanted to know something more specific:

Anne: What do you really love in life? What are your goals?

Joe: Ooh, a deep question. I love these. You go first though – I want to hear your thoughts.

Joe simply flips the question on its head. By saying "you first" he makes an implicit promise that he will answer the question, but only after she offers her answer first. It in no way makes Joe look bad, but it shows that he is confident and in charge of the conversation.

146

Of course, this method of deference doesn't always work. People sometimes don't understand what they want out of the conversation any more than you do and you'll need to answer their questions to stay involved, but trust me – the more you can control the flow of information, the better it will flow.

Politics or Religion

Nothing can ruin a perfectly good conversation faster than an ideological difference on something highly opinionated like politics or religion.

Sometimes, this can be avoided by just never mentioning the topic, but you can't control what someone else says, so if suddenly they say something you completely disagree with, you'll need to take a step to either staunch the damage or move away from the conversation altogether.

Martina: I just saw the debates for the governor race. I can't believe they want to raise taxes.

Steve: It's an interesting development for sure. I'm not sure what I think of it yet; I'll have to read a bit more.

It's a total copout, but it works if you really don't want to discuss the issue. If you're a strong supporter of the candidate that wants to raise taxes, the issue might be hard to ignore, but I strongly urge you not to let a small disagreement on policy ruin a new relationship.

Remember to change the subject quickly if you're really uncomfortable talking about it – most people will carry on with controversial topics until something else comes up to distract them.

This goes double for religion. Most of the time, you will find that people won't push religion on you unless it is a very prominent part of their identity. So if someone does bring up religion and you either disagree or would just rather not talk about it, you have options:

It's a deferral but it works because you make a small, safe joke. If it still manages to upset the person you're talking to, you may not be able to talk about religion at all.

The Art of the Question

Nothing is more intimate or potentially engaging than a question. When someone asks the right question, they immediately attract attention and interest from their conversation partner.

And vice versa, when someone asks the wrong question, people get annoyed and try to get out of a conversation. It also happens to be one of only two ways to truly start a conversation – you either ask someone a question or you state a fact, and in my experience, asking questions is far more effective in opening the mind of whoever you're trying to talk to.

So, how do you ask a question in a way that will draw someone toward you and convince them that you're interesting enough to actually answer?

First, you need to make at least a basic observation about the person you're meeting. Again, remember not to make any assumptions.

You shouldn't ask questions like "how many months pregnant are you?" if you're not 100% sure the woman is pregnant. You shouldn't ask a police officer what his quota is unless you know he has a sense of humor. It's dangerous ground and generally very rude.

On the other hand, asking someone about their suit or the food they're eating at a buffet or the book they're reading are perfect openers that use existing information to generate a direct connection and help you get into character.

Knowing When to End the Conversation

This is a tricky one. Some people (myself included) can strike up a conversation and let it roar throughout – intriguing anyone we meet, soliciting laughs and generating rapport left, right and sideways – but when we need to end the conversation, things get awkward.

This is a problem I had for a long time, well after I developed much of what you see in this book. But, I learned something very simple, and seemingly counter intuitive about the end of a conversation.

You should end a conversation before it reaches its natural apex. It may feel like there are dozens more things to say, but before you know it, you'll both be tapped and the crickets will start chirping.

So, it's your job to take initiative and end a conversation as soon as possible, before anything gets awkward and you need to back away uncomfortably.

Avoiding Cliché

One of the most common conversation killers in my experience is the age old cliché. Pretty much anything you say that sounds silly or recycled is going to pull you both out of the conversation and lead to an uncomfortable silence. The last thing you want is to kill the flow of conversation when it was going so nicely.

To avoid clichés, stick to topics that you can offer original opinions on and try not to sum anything up in a single sentence or phrase. While clichés are bad, remember that jokes can be endearing. If you can make a joke out of a cliché or catchphrase from pop culture, go for it – people will love it.

"Storytelling is my currency. It's my only worth. The only thing of value I have in this life is my ability to tell a story, whether in print, orating, writing it down or having people acting it out.

-- Kevin Smith

If you sit and have a conversation with a master, you'll notice one thing above all else – they know how to tell a darn good story. Someone with the ability to tell stories about seemingly any topic with gusto is generally the most likable people in the room.

They draw attention to themselves like flies to honey as men and women lean closer to learn about their wayward microwave or their uncannily intelligent dog.

But, it's not a secret genetic trait; it's a skill and anyone can learn how to do it. It just takes practice and a careful ear for what's interesting. Engaging hooks, humorous anecdotes, careful retelling and the ability to cut out the details that just plain don't matter will all make your stories infinitely more engaging.

They don't need to be deep or highly entertaining. You don't need to make up trips to the Antarctic or hiking trips into Everest – you just need to be yourself and let your natural humor and energy flow into every story you tell.

What to Talk About

First up, let me say that you can tell a story about *anything*. Literally anything that has happened to you can be an effective story. Should you tell a story about anything? Probably not, but with the right approach, it's definitely possible. So, with that in mind, how do you choose the perfect scenarios to entertain the people you meet on a daily basis?

To start with, leave behind the super entertaining stories you've cultivated from a young age. We all have those trump card stories – the ones we've been sharing since High School that are so interesting people cannot help but listen. They're great, but they don't work as well in casual conversation. First up, they rarely leave an opening for someone to respond with their own details. If you describe how you went cliff diving in the Andes, other people will definitely be intrigued, but they may also be intimidated into silence.

150

Alternately, they may become competitive and you must work to out-tell them and their story. In both cases, you have an unwanted situation. So, the alternative is to work toward creating entertaining stories out of pretty much nothing. Don't abandon your trump cards. You'll need them for first dates or award presentations, but don't use them on a daily basis either. It's just plain lazy storytelling.

Hooks and Pauses

Okay, now, with your boring, normal every day story in mind, it's time to put it together in a way that will be interesting and engaging. We do that with hooks and pauses. Don't start by saying "I have this funny story about this thing that happened to me this morning" - it's dull. Instead, say "Guess what a microwave, my three year old Beagle and my left dress shoe have in common?"

Who could honestly resist wanting to know more about whatever happened between your Beagle, shoe and microwave? If you dig a little deeper, it's probably a pretty dull story if told wrong, but when announced in such an interesting way, people will eat it up.

Hooks are great, but you must also tell your story with the right degree of balance and pauses. Listen to a speech by any politician (the party doesn't matter). They will stop for half beats, drag out important words, give meaningful glances, and use their hand gestures to create an entire discussion out of just a few hundred words.

Your story should benefit from the same powerful rhetorical tools. Know when to stop and hold the attention of your reader, when to lead to a new point, or when to pull back and leave someone guessing what happens next.

Editing for Content

Of course, this leads directly to my next point – you shouldn't tell everyone everything about a story. If you tell a story about your dog, a microwave and a shoe, there are probably a LOT of details in there that just don't matter.

Even if you tell the story in an interesting, funny, engaging matter, there should still be a switch in your mind somewhere that you know when to flip to shut down the stuff that just isn't that interesting.

How do you do that? By framing every part of your story in terms of how you *feel about it or react to it.* This is a simple strategy used be advertising executives for decades to help prospective buyers connect to a story on a visceral level. Someone might hear your story, understand the points and still not care very much because it doesn't affect them.

However, if you tell the same story by describing how you felt about each part of the story, they can connect to you in the present and engage with the story through natural empathy. It works in almost every conversation. Some people don't connect very well with others, and that will make the process harder in some cases, but it's relatively rare in social situations.

I know this concept is a bit complicated, so let me show you what I mean. Below are two stories – one told as unedited account of what happened this morning when I ate breakfast and another as I would actually tell the story to a group of strangers I just met at a conference:

Example A:

Oh, hey, a funny thing happened to me this morning when I was eating breakfast. I decided I wanted to eat something at least a little healthy so I went out and got some Chex and then some bananas to put in the Chex. I then realized I didn't have any milk so I had to go back to the store. I got home and realized my bananas had gone bad, so I went to the store one more time to get bananas. When I was at the store, I got stuck in line behind these five people who were together but all buying their groceries separately. It took like twenty minutes to get through the line and even then, I still had to walk home. By the time I got back home, I had five minutes until I needed to leave so I ate a donut and caught the bus.

Example B:

I have a heck of a time eating healthily for breakfast. Take today for example. For all intents and purposes, I was going to eat something healthy. I jumped out of bed, did some calisthenics (do a mock stretch here), headed to store and got some cereal for a healthy, early morning breakfast. Guess what...not a drop of milk in the house. Not sure if Suzy drank it all (my dog – I'm pretending they already know who she is), but without thumbs it would be a heck of a trick to reach the handle on the fridge. Fast forward twenty minutes, I'm standing in line at the grocery store behind five tourists with bulky neon green fanny packs, five separate orders of food, and traveler's checks with lots of fancy European symbols on them. I felt bad for them because the cashier was a little rude, but I was in a hurry, so I had to abandon my milk run and jog home. Try as I might, I ended up with a Chocolate Éclair in my stomach as I headed to the bus. I feel bad for not eating healthy, but my taste buds sure aren't complaining.

See the difference?

Exhibit A is pretty dull and straightforward. It reads more like a police report than a story. The second example is a bit longer (normally I shorten it up), but it's more interesting too. I describe what I saw, how I felt about it, and interject cute details like my dog, which opens up all new strains of conversation. At no point am I forcing anything, and at no point do I complain (another big no-no in a new conversation), but I manage to outline a relatively amusing story from my morning.

We all have stories like this every single day. Imagine how easy conversation will become when you can whip out a new one of these whenever you need to. You don't need to rack your brain for something interesting or topically related – just describe anything in your life and people will draw from it whatever they like. It's actually kind of fun once you get the hang of it.

Common Responses to Embarrassing Situations

I won't sugar coat things for you – there will be situations in which you get embarrassed. It just happens.

What really matters is not what other people think of you in these situations, but how you respond to them in the first place. If you react properly and keep from making things worse, trust me – you'll get away with far fewer scrapes and bruises than if you tried to cover up it all up.

Because we've all been there and the world is filled with stories about embarrassment, there is an endless well of examples to draw from. Here are a few situations and ways to get out of them tactfully:

Jokes About Sex – Some people have flappy jaws and will say whatever comes to mind. Jokes about sex related to you can be extremely embarrassing, especially if the crowd is inappropriate. To handle these situations, let the joke pass, cover it up, or throw something back.

Exes in the Room – If you run into an ex, the easiest way to handle the situation is to be calm and go about your business. If they talk to you, be polite and act as though nothing is a big deal. The only time these moments become truly embarrassing is if you treat it as anything but a run of the mill encounter.

Falling Down, Dropping Something, General Clumsiness – When you make a goof, spill a drink, fall on our face or otherwise show off your clumsiness, be good natured. Brush yourself off, laugh a little and make sure people know that you're okay with it.

Using the Wrong Name for Someone You Just Met – This is a tough one. People will be extremely put off when you can't remember their name. The easiest way to handle this is to apologize, explain why it happened and if you have the composure, tell a joke. That might prove tough, but it's not impossible if you focus hard enough. Embarrassment is part of the human experience. You may not like it, expect it, or know how to handle it, but it will happen.

The best advice I can give you is to not let it affect your future. If you constantly simmer and think on the time you embarrassed yourself in front of a date, you'll never be successful on your next date or networking event.

Use everything I've taught you thus far to push it out of your mind and get over the feeling that failure is imminent. Those moments can make good stories.

Pushing the Interaction

Commonly enough, we do the bare minimum when we meet someone new for the first time. It's hard to go outside your comfort zone and work toward providing something more than what's expected.

What do I mean by "expected"? Basically, we're talking about simple pleasantries. Two people meet, they say hi, they talk about a few mundane details, maybe pass a compliment back and forth and then go their separate ways.

You do it every day with the grocery store clerk and the people in your office. But, actual communication – the kind that will help elicit new friendships and build relationships – requires you to go beyond just "saying hi" and actually pushing the interaction to a different level.

Getting Someone Interested in Your Point of View

I've provided a number of tips to developing rapport, building a relationship and creating a lasting, positive first impression, but how do you get someone to actively want more information about your point of view? You offer value in the conversation.

Give more than you receive, without giving away so much that you appear needy. It's a tricky balancing act at first but as you practice, you'll quickly find that you're a natural at making people want more.

Value is a tricky word to use when talking about a conversation, but it works for good reason. People think in terms of what they get out of any given situation.

Sure, most people get over the selfishness after they get to know you a bit, but the whole point is that we're talking about people you've just met for the first time. And when you first meet someone, you ask yourself, "What do I get out of talking to this person?"

That's where you need to make your statement – preferably as early in the conversation as possible. The goal is to show them that continuing to talk to you is going to be good for them in some way.

It varies depending on the type of conversation you're having what this actually means, of course. Here are some examples:

On a Date – When you're on a date and someone comes into it thinking "what's there for me?" you'd better be prepared to show off your best qualities. That means being funny, being interesting, and being empathetic. We've talked about all of these qualities in the book so far; it shouldn't be hard to engage someone on a personal level in a way that will show them how caring and interested you are, but if you don't do that, they will quickly wonder what the point is.

Work Conversation – At work, the concept of value is a little different. When networking with someone, the immediate concern is that the other person can provide as much value as they get. For example, if the owner of a restaurant and a lawyer meet up at a bar, they both need to feel they could benefit from the conversation. The restaurant owner should need legal advice and the lawyer should need a new client (and possibly some free food). If the lawyer has a full case load and the restaurant owner already has a lawyer, they won't be able to connect on a professional level. They could be best buddies otherwise, but the situation doesn't call for that kind of interaction.

Value in a conversation is a tough thing to determine. A lot of people (myself included) don't like to think in those terms, but unfortunately, most other people do.

So, you need to work at an early stage to show the other person that by talking to you, they will receive not only an interesting new connection, but someone who can provide something they need. Ideally, if you become friends later, you'll both get past this give-take relationship, but for now, it's part of the process.

What it does right now is it shows the other person that you have something they may be interested in. By following their verbal, physical and kinaesthetic cues, you can learn exactly what things you say are interesting and what things are boring to them.

You shouldn't change your conversational tactics completely just to fit their responses, but you can start to tweak and adjust them, to avoid topics they are uninterested in and talk up those that they show interest in.

The Foundation Bridge Principle

Whether you want to create a closer friendship with someone just met, turn a business colleague into a business partner or turn your friendship into something more, the Foundation Bridge Principle is one of the most powerful ways you can experience and build rapport with everyone you meet (which is why I gave it its own mini section, so pay attention!)

People react from an emotional place.

If you can trigger an emotion or feeling in them, they'll feel a connection to you—and when it comes to being well liked, that's exactly what you're going for.

The Foundation Bridge Principle is based upon storytelling, and then eases into a personal connection. Let's say that you've been invited to a happy hour. You're colleagues will all be, including your boss, and his assistant who you've been eyeing for a while now.

Now, you could sit in the background, listening to everyone talk more than you're talking yourself (in which you'll feel invisible, and you are sick and tired of feeling invisible) or you can join the conversation and bring a whole new level of connection the group hasn't come across in years.

The Foundation Bridge Principle involves telling a story to engage people and attract them to you.

So, if the group is talking about the latest pitch the made to a best-selling author, you could tell a story about that one time you bumped into a best-selling author and dropped your glass of wine all over their white pants.

Smile while you tell that story, or laugh at your clumsiness. Chances are, your audience (who you've now captivated with your wit and charming story) will encourage them to join in and tell a story of their own.

Before you know it, you'll achieved a connection to others than before this story, you just worked with. But, now that you've told a story they like and were emotionally drawn to (through the effective Foundation Bridge Principle), you know have a group of co-workers who you work with, and are FRIENDS with.

Exercises and Questions

1. Make a list of possible social outings you can do in the next 2-3 weeks and make a commitment to attend at least one per week.

2. Create a list of time frames for socializing in a notebook. The first time you go to a party or a bar, commit to at least 15 minutes and conversation with one person. Move up from there to 30 minutes and beyond.

3. Write down three embarrassing memories you have of social interactions. Now, consciously ignore them whenever they pop up in a social setting.

4. Go out one day this week and only pay attention to the cues people use in conversation. Try to determine if someone is an audible, visual, or kinaesthetic thinker.

5. Practice mirroring the posture and actions of a friend and ask them afterwards if it was obvious. Work toward a comfortable medium between mirroring and them realizing your actions.

6. Write down five icebreakers you would like to use for a new conversation and take notes on how those conversations proceed.

7. Write down three mundane things that happened to you today. Now, make an interesting story out of each. Record it and play it back tomorrow to see if it is still interesting.

8. Record three things you can do to provide direct value to someone you've just met.

9. On a scale of 1-10 how comfortable are you in a 1 on 1 conversation?

1. 2. 3. 4. 5. 6. 7. 8. 9. 10

10. If you rated it less than a 5, write down specific actions you've taken away from this chapter that you can perform to improve your rating.

Chapter Nine:

Meeting People

"...the only people for me are the mad ones, the ones who are mad to live, mad to talk, mad to be saved, desirous of everything at the same time, the ones who never yawn or say a commonplace thing, but burn, burn, burn like fabulous yellow roman candles exploding like spiders across the stars..."

– Jack Kerouac, author of On The Road

With a smoother, more confident approach to how you interact with the men and women you meet, now is the time to take it up a notch and actually go out and meet them.

But, where and how do you do this? That will depend partly on the type of people you want to meet, what your interests are and what you hope to get out of any new relationships you create.

For instance, if you want to meet a man or woman for romantic tryst, you'll want to go where the men or women you're aiming to meet are located. If you want to meet academic friends, a book club or community college course would be a good way to meet those types of people. It's all in what you hope to get out of your interactions.

10 Step Process to Meeting Someone for the First Time

This list may not apply to every man and woman out there, but it will give a solid foundation on which to build a new conversation and hopefully build a new relationship out of.

Make Eye Contact and Gauge Interest – First of all, make sure someone looks interested in talking to you. Take a peek at them from across the room, look them in the eye, smile or wave. Basically, get a measure of their presence at the moment. If they look away, ignore you, or simply look uncomfortable, rethink your approach. Maybe in a little bit when they have loosened up some.

Introduce Yourself – If you get the green light or simply feel like drawing someone into conversation, go for it. Head over, say hi, use an icebreaker or two and tell a joke. Basically, whatever conversational style you feel most comfortable with is a good way to open.

Make Small Talk and Develop Understanding of their Conversational Style – In the first five minutes or so, you should aim to understand as much as you can about their conversational style as possible. Are they visual, audible, or kinaesthetic? Are they storytellers or listeners? Do they want to talk about work, personal details, or something else entirely? Listen closely in those early moments whenever they talk and start mirroring their approach to the conversation.

Build Rapport – Hopefully in those first few moments you'll have tapped into the natural rapport any two likeminded individuals share upon meeting. Now, it's time to build on that rapport by mirroring their conversational style, building on topics they clearly like and increasing how it all progresses.

Tell a Story or Generate Interest – Make sure to give away a few small details about yourself in the course of conversation. All the niceties in the world do you no good if you fail to draw them into your world a bit. They won't open up until they feel comfortable and that requires you to show at least some of your cards. Tell a personal story, mention your family in passing, describe your dog – get something out there that they couldn't learn just by observing you naturally.

Gauge When to End the Conversation - Within 5-10 minutes, start gauging when it's best to end a conversation. Most arenas designed for meeting people practically demand that you keep any single conversation short as you move on to talk to other people. If you stay with someone too long, you risk appearing clingy or worse yet, overstaying your welcome and boring them. If they really enjoy your presence, they'll seek you out again later.

Push the Conversation to the Next Level – If you and your new acquaintance really hit it off, don't cut it too short. Push the conversation to the next level by separating from the pack, discussing something more in depth or developing further rapport. If you're in a dating environment, separate from the crowd to get some privacy.

Get Contact Information – Ultimately, if you meet someone you like, get their contact information. It's not weird to ask someone for their business card or email address, especially if you hit it off. If it's someone of the opposite gender, play your cards a little more carefully. Keep it casual and make it an afterthought to ask for their contact information. A good trick is to have them enter their email or phone number into your phone directly. They can then touch something of yours, and will be far more likely to provide a real detail.

Wrap Up – Finally, when the conversation is winding down, make additional pleasantries and wind it down. Do this by summing up the conversation, giving a nice compliment as to the conversational quality and telling them you'll talk soon. Never say goodbye in a final tone. Instead say something like "see you soon" or "talk to you soon" or "we'll probably bump into each other again soon". These create an open- ended nature to your relationship and make it easy to pick up where you left off when you meet again.

Walk Away – As hard as it may be, eventually you must walk away from the conversation. Don't feel bad or apologize, just let them know you'd like to talk to other people or that you need to check on your friends. If you do it casually, no one will take it the wrong way. Just make sure you've wrapped up whatever conversational strain you're on and never cut them off. It's rude and won't make for an easy pick up point when you run back into each other.

If you do it right, your conversation will grow and run its course as naturally as any other interaction. You don't need to force anything, and should avoid anything that makes either of you feel awkward. Do all that and you'll be set going forward.

Nervous? You're Not Alone

Nervousness is a natural response to an uncomfortable situation. Consider for a moment what really happens when you meet someone for the first time, on a primal level. You walk up to a stranger and deep in your brain a switch stands at the ready between Fight and Flight – the classic response to a tense situation.

Your body grows tense, you start to sweat and your brain starts to race. This will continue until the threat has been analysed and negated or until you retreat from it altogether, neither of which will happen for a few moments – hence nervousness.

But, while our bodies may be confused about what meeting a new person means, you shouldn't be. It's an opportunity. Even when meeting someone you know might be difficult, see it as a challenge, not as a potential problem. Realistically, conversation and socialization are tools we use to excel in the world – things that can set us apart – and not threats to analyse and run away from.

As your confidence builds and you gain experience in conversation and meeting new people, you'll get a far better understanding of how this works. Part of it is practice and another part is perspective. With time you'll gain both and hopefully blow the people you meet out of the water.

Parties

The party is an interesting phenomenon. Dozens of people from different backgrounds and interests get together in a neutral setting and celebrate an event that likely only affects a small number of attendees.

In short, you'll be tossed into a fishbowl with a lot of other people who also don't know anyone and may feel uncomfortable too.

So, the key to successfully meeting people in a party and coming off as the slick new likable guy you've been aiming for is to offer a comforting presence to the people who are in the same boat as you.

If it's your party or you know the people for whom the party is being thrown, this is a lot easier, but even if you're a complete stranger, the magnetic party persona works just as well.

Worried that someone will call you on your bravado? If you're honest and confident in your own presence, the worst that can happen is someone else will develop a problem with you – it's not your issue. They have a problem and you cannot solve it. They need to do that for themselves.

Party Etiquette

Parties are tough and the fact that as you get older, they tend to require a certain degree of etiquette certainly doesn't make any of it any easier. So, when it comes time to go to a party, make sure you do a little research before coming in.

If you're going to a mixer at a bar or someone's loft, the odds are that there are no "rules". You should ask about bringing food or drink, but beyond that just try to look nice and make sure you don't drink too much.

However, for more elegant, formal parties, problems can develop. Here are a few of the etiquette issues you may run into at a formal dinner party:

Dress Code – What you wear can be a little tough. The easiest way to figure out what you're supposed to wear is to simply ask someone. There are dozens of codes and everyone interprets them differently, so like anything else, don't overthink it – just ask someone what they would do.

How to Eat Your Meal – Most dinner parties are not this formal, but if it happens, follow the lead of someone nearby. You'll see other people using the proper forks or spoons and you should simply follow along. Mirroring in this situation is a fantastic way to get it right.

Giving Toasts – If you have to give a toast, make sure you have a clear idea of what you'll say. If it's a formal toast, such as at a wedding, write it ahead of time and put it on cards. Avoid too much alcohol and make sure you're ready for whatever happens.

What to Bring – Always ask before bringing anything to a party. A bottle of wine is often traditional, while food is usually not expected. However, if the party is less formal than expected, you may want to have something on hand just in case.

In short, don't let the formality of a dinner party or even the social tensions of a casual party stress you out. There are a plenty of other people there who also have no idea what they are doing. You're in good company.

Chapter Ten:

How to Act Around Strangers

"Nothing is impossible, the word itself says 'I'm possible'!"

— Audrey Hepburn

Being around large groups of people can be tough for a few reasons.

First, you have to talk to a lot of people. Second, most of those people are perfect strangers. Not a fun prospect for someone just learning the social skills needed to impress people. But, luckily for you, there are ways to get around this constant, seemingly unrelenting sensation of "what do I do now?"

Progressive Exposure

In her book, *Good-Bye to Shy* Leil Lowndes approaches shyness and discomfort in social settings as psychologists approach very real phobias. The idea being that diving headfirst into a situation you are terrified of will only create greater fear and reinforce your aversion to social activities.

We've already gone through a number of coping strategies – the tools used by those psychologists to calm your mind and prepare it to enter that situation. By reducing stress, preparing conversation pieces, and building an approach that allows you to be confident in yourself, you're prepared to tackle that which scares you most – strangers.

Now it's time for progressive exposure – the process of slowing putting yourself into increasingly scary situations. Here's an example (apologies in advance if you're afraid of spiders). Say Will has arachnophobia and is therefore terrified of spiders – not just a little creeped out, by physically terrified to the point of full blown anxiety attacks.

So, it would be a bad idea to lock Will in a room with spiders to "get over" it. Yes, you're supposed to confront your fears, but having a heart attack sure isn't going to help.

So, through progressive exposure, Will starts by looking at a picture of a spider that is too small to make out.

Then after a week or so of occasionally viewing pictures, he might watch a video of spiders moving around.

Once Will grows comfortable with that, he could see an actual spider, in the zoo or in a cage at a pet store.

Will might never get to the point that a spider on his skin doesn't cause severe fear, but he will likely weaken those fears a LOT and may get over it to the point of being okay with them in his home eating the other bugs.

Another example (with less creepy crawlies) is Samantha. She's terrified of going on roller coasters at the amusement park. But, because she loves her children, she agrees to get on the teacup ride. And after a few turns on the teacups, she's okay getting on the tilta-whirl. Eventually, even though Samantha is still terrified of the roller coaster, it's not quite as big of a deal to get on it and she can at least set foot in the line and make it through a ride for the little ones.

The point of all this is that it works just as well for you and your fear of social interaction as it does for Will and spiders or Samantha and her roller coaster.

The idea is that instead of saying to yourself "I need to be at this party for X amount of time so that I can develop a strong connection with all these people," and subsequently stressing yourself out about the prospect of spending so much time with strangers, you devote only a few minutes to it. This works just as well in conversation as it does in actually attending the party.

Go into a party thinking "I will stick around for 15 minutes, and I will talk to at least one person I don't know." That's all you need to do – it's hard, but it's manageable and you can then get out of there and go hyperventilate in the comfort of your car.

As it turns out, you'll find that 15 minutes and one stranger aren't that bad. You can still leave after 15 minutes, but the next time you go to a party, you'll be able to handle 30 minutes and 2 or 3 strangers.

Another good tip from Lowndes' playbook is to take a friend with you to the party. This is a must in my opinion.

Going to a party on your own is a sure- fire way to generate more stress than is generally considered healthy. You'll push yourself too far, feel the pressure to perform in front of people you don't know, and eventually become overwhelmed by the prospect of having to talk to more strangers.

With a friend in tow, you have an anchor who you can return to when you grow uncomfortable.

Make sure your friend is of the same sex, especially if you're currently single – you won't want anyone thinking you're unavailable if you really are. It completely changes the dynamic of your conversations and will make it very hard to connect with the opposite sex.

Working the Room

The very idea of getting in there and actively "working the room" might make your heart skip a beat or two, but remember our game plan. You'll aim for just one or two new people at a time. It might be weeks before you attend enough parties that you'll need to talk to multiple people at the same time. That makes things a little easier, at least to get yourself started.

But, when it comes time to get in there and talk to dozens of people in succession without breaking stride, how do you do it? How do you maintain the likable new personality we've crafted over the course of this book and wow everyone you meet?

First, take a deep breath and relax. The single biggest thing you can do right now is step back and calm down – let yourself relax and feel the comfort that you've developed in talking to any one person. Now, what exactly is different about interacting with a guy you meet at a party versus one you meet at your office or the grocery store?

Bars

A bar is one of the most commonly visited social settings. Unfortunately, it can also be one of the most frustrating. There are a few reasons why.

To start with, you either drink or you don't. If you do drink, all the hard work you've put in on your confidence and body language is much harder to recall. It's not impossible, but the loss of inhibition and motor controls can severely damage your first impressions. And for those who do not drink, everything seems just a bit sillier when you're sober.

So, to get the most out of a bar, you need to have a specific goal in mind and set limits for yourself – both in what you are willing to drink and what you're willing to put up with from other people.

Sitting there in a "deep" conversation with someone who has had entirely too much to drink is not going to be a lot of fun and will likely leave you high and dry at the end of the night.

Go with Friends

Much like at a party, friends can make bar hopping infinitely easier. They offer a safe haven when things get awkward, an instant excuse when you need to end a conversation, and a ripcord if you need to get out of the bar or club immediately. That said, try not to rely too heavily on your friends to keep you going through a long evening at a bar or club.

They probably want to socialize too and don't need you inundating them repeatedly with your insecurities and concerns about what Susie or Jimmie or Tom think about you. I know it sounds harsh, but I'm looking out for your own wellbeing. Friends won't want to come with you to a bar if you cling to them like Saran wrap all night.

So, force yourself out of your comfort zone and get out there to meet people.

Be Interesting

Everything in this guide has built up to this moment and the simple act of being a more interesting conversation partner.

So, when I say to "be interesting" in conversation, I hope you have a good idea of what I mean. The brain may go blank, but the tips should all be there still, bouncing around in your head, ready to be put to use. Here are some refreshers just in case:

Don't Get Drunk – Drunkenness may be funny sometimes but it's rarely interesting, especially if the people you meet are sober. We'll talk more about alcohol soon, but for now, keep your intake as moderated as possible to avoid any embarrassing outbursts.

Don't Be Afraid to Share – Tell people about yourself and be proud of what you have to say. Every time I go to a bar, I'll inevitably end up in a conversation with someone that starts with "What do you do for a living?" and it's amazing how many people will gladly label themselves and be done with it. Describe what you do, give them a story and show them why what you do is as interesting as you think it is. And if it's not interesting, don't put yourself down – tell a story that illustrates the diversity of your job. Every position can be described this way if you know how to go about it.

Ask Educated Questions – Get in there and ask questions about the people you meet, but make sure they are educated based on the rest of the conversation. It shows that you're listening, and that you have something to add to any part of the conversation.

A bar conversation is usually pretty simple. It's loud in there, people have been drinking at least a little bit, and there are plenty of distractions (again alcohol and usually TVs). So you don't need to discuss Thoreau or the nature of existence, but you should try to be as engaging as possible within the constraints of the room and the atmosphere.

Clubs and Meet-up Groups

Personally, I think one of the best ways to meet people, whether you're looking for a new friend or a date, is to join up with clubs and meet up groups in your areas of interest. Then, you don't have to pretend or research to be interested in what other people enjoy. If you meet someone at a soccer outing who is into soccer, there's a good chance you have a love of soccer in common – otherwise why would you both be at a soccer outing?

But, finding these meet-up groups is often easier said than done. The Internet makes things easier, but it is still pretty hit or miss as to whether you'll enjoy yourself or find the type of group you're actually looking for. Be prepared for a few disappointments as you look for the ideal outings to hone your social skills.

Joining Existing Groups

Groups are all over the place, but you need to have an in before you just jump into them.

Technology simplifies this quite a bit, allowing you to essentially inject yourself into a group with the click of a button. But, even if you do this, make sure to develop a sense of your value to the group before meeting people.

For example, if you meet people on Facebook or Meetup.com and want to join them at their next official gathering, make sure to email or chat with at least one other member so you have a pillar you can rely on when you go to the event. It will make your life much easier in getting to know people and building rapport.

Everyone enjoys their hobbies in different ways and more often than not people who get together at these hobby-centric events are very invested in what they're doing. You may be just a casual practitioner – most people won't judge you for that, but it can put a strain in how you discuss things with your new friends.

Meetup.com

Meetup.com is built exactly for this purpose and it takes quite a bit of the awkwardness out of these meetings. People are inherently comfortable because more often than not no one knows anyone else and the roster rolls change over so fast that you'll very rarely be the only new person in the group.

To join a Meetup group, visit the website and sign up as a new member. It's completely free unless you plan on creating your own Meetup group, in which case it costs $19 per month. Some Meetups may cost money too, but that will always be posted on the group's page by the organizer.

Make sure to provide as many details as you can when signing up. I recommend adding a photo as well. Photographs are good to personalize your membership and provide a pre- introduction.

People are also more likely to recognize you when they meet-up with you in real life.

Once you've signed up for the site, you can join any open groups and apply to join others. Some Meetup groups require you to be approved by an Organizer or to pay a small fee for the Meetups. The best part, though, is that you are under no obligation to attend a Meetup event or even meet anyone until you're comfortable with it.

If the group has three meetings a month and you have skipped 12 of them, no one will know. In fact, most of these groups have attendance to member ratios of 1:10 or higher. A lot of people join these groups and very few of them actually participate.

That may seem disheartening, but it will open you up to do pretty much whatever you want in the comfortable confines of your digital profile.

Book Clubs

One of the most common and oldest forms of groups is the book club. A book club is essentially when a group of 5-15 people, or sometimes more, reads the same book over the course of a month or two and then gets together to discuss it.

Think college English but without any grades and with books you actually want to read.

Book clubs are not for everyone, but if you like to read and want the challenge of speaking up in a group of people, you'll have plenty of opportunities to do both in a book club.

Meetup.com is loaded with book clubs if you want to join one cold and meet up with people. Alternately, you can find groups at many independent book stores or on websites like LibraryThing.com where they are organized by readers in every conceivable genre.

And before you think that most book clubs only read the latest Oprah selection or something from 9th grade literature, know that there are all types of book clubs.

I have been part of science fiction, children's lit, post-apocalyptic fiction, poetry, and translated book clubs and they were all full of interesting people and very interesting books.

Starting Your Own Groups

Starting your own group takes a good amount of ambition, organizing power, and the ability to get people to follow your lead in as many ways as possible.

In short, you'll need to have mastered quite a few of the tips in this book and already be putting them to good use in all aspects of your social life.

But, starting your own group gives you quite a few things. First, it ensures you meet a lot of people. If you join a group that meets with 20 people every two weeks, the odds are that you won't get to know all of those people very well.

As the leader of the group, it's your job to introduce yourself, maintain order, and be on good terms with every member of the group.

If leadership is something you gravitate towards, and your new likability is in need of a test, take a leap and try starting your own group in this fashion. It's not easy, but it can be very rewarding.

Internet Meetings

Speaking of the Internet, there is always the opportunity to meet new people online.

Despite the long standing stigma over online meetings and interactions, more and more people are finding it easier to be themselves in a digital setting, prior to meeting up with a potential friend or romantic interest in person.

How you handle online meetings really isn't that much different than the offline variety, but I do have one important tip for you.

Remember, unless you are using a webcam so you and the other person can see each other, there are a lot of unspoken inflections and body language quirks that go into a conversation. As a result, if you word something awkwardly in an email or chat message, it's very easy for someone to take it completely the wrong way.

Gaming – In recent years, online gaming has become an extremely popular way to meet new people, generate relationships and stay social when all else fails. It can also be a crutch so I warn you to approach online gaming with the requisite care to ensure you don't get addicted and that you maintain a decent distance from the barrage of stimuli. In short, don't get lost in this world. It's not good for you.

Forums – Forums are a great way to discuss topics that have great meaning to you or that you have a lot of opinions about. A site like big-boards.com contains thousands of forum threads on almost any topic you can imagine. Go there and you'll find hundreds of opportunities to join in conversations about your hobbies, ask questions about new endeavours, or simply get to know people you may be interested in.

Social Networking – Social networking used to be a niche opportunity to meet people. Now, it's the largest single activity on the Internet and it represents a chance to get out there and meet pretty much anyone you could imagine. There are groups on Facebook, lists on Twitter, and images and videos on Flickr or

YouTube. Again, be careful with social networking. It's incredibly addictive, and if you're not careful it can draw you in with both the social *and* gaming aspects of online interaction. My rule for social networking is always "if you *can* meet in the real world, do." Use Facebook to stay in touch with people across the country or overseas, but don't have a conversation with someone who is three miles away – get out and have coffee or something.

This stuff is tricky – playing around online opens up all sorts of black holes in conversation. All the stuff I told you about body language, cue reading, and voice tone? Yeah, that's all out the window now because it's impossible to determine from text.

Even with webcams, the technology is a bit sketchy still to allow for perfect interaction. So, I still recommend in-person meeting whenever possible, but if you're in a rural area, or you simply need a way to ease into meeting people, this will get you there.

Meeting Internet Friends Offline So, what happens when you have a new friend on Facebook and they want to meet up with you somewhere along the way? Do you just set a time and meet them without a second guess? In some cases that can work well enough, but with the way things work these days, I tend to urge caution.

First, make sure you know at least a few basics about the person you're meeting and then verify those details.

If they are unwilling to pass on their name and phone number, then you probably shouldn't be meeting with them yet.

Look them up in Google, check any stories they tell you against online references and make sure they are for real. Don't graduate this to stalking – it's pretty creepy when you know things about them that they have not yet shared – but make sure they're legit. This is doubly important if you're going on a date.

As for the meeting place, make sure it's a public place where you'll both feel comfortable. A coffee shop is a safe, clichéd location that most people will gladly agree to. You should also try to have a good signal for meeting up.

How to Be Likable Online

So, how do you take everything you've learned in this book and convert it to online interactions? That's a tough one. Not only do you not have the benefit of seeing each other, you lose a lot of inflection and tone in an email. So, if you've never actually met anyone before, things like sarcasm, jokes, and questions can go over poorly in written words.

To keep from making big snafus in your messages, practice what I call careful typing. I'm sure you've seen the gibberish that many people use for writing emails to each other in modern society.

It's a mess and often doesn't make any sense.

I don't want to date myself too much, but it's ridiculous watching some young people attempt communication in email. Most of the disagreements you see on message boards and blogs is due to poor communication skills, not an actual ideological disagreement.

So, when you write a message to someone, use complete sentences, clearly state your thoughts and make sure you're statements are well formed. Don't write a formal letter to a stranger – it will likely make them uncomfortable – but also don't write things in bits and spurts either.

Another tip to being likable online is to make sure you're open without being too open. Remember how you're supposed to toss out a good amount of details about your life to people you just met to create rapport.

The same goes online, but I recommend you steer clear of things like family members, where you live, or details they could use to learn more about you than you'd like.

It may sound paranoid, but the risk of being manipulated or stalked online is always there – far more so than with a stranger you just met in person. Anonymity does strange things to people. Don't give them a chance to test those boundaries and things will remain safe and sound.

Sports

I already talked about meet-up groups and clubs, but sports in particular can be a very effective way to meet new people. Remember the camaraderie you feel when you and a few of your classmates would team up for 20 minutes in gym class for a game of basketball or football? It's exactly the same as an adult, except with far more opportunities to extend those interactions outside the playing field.

Community Leagues

Most cities and towns have some form of social league you can join for sports. The problem for most people is finding a league that fits their athletic skill level.

If you're just interested in meeting people, it can be hard to find a purely social league with minimally non-competitive people.

For this, I recommend looking for sports that don't breed that hyper-competitive nature. Kickball and ultimate Frisbee are both very good options if they are available in your area.

Finding social leagues for softball and soccer is feasible too, but make sure to vet the league first. If you're not sure, there is always a risk that it is a more competitive than you're ready for and that you'll be uncomfortable pushing yourself that much.

Putting Leagues Together

Creating your own league is a bit harder than just joining one. Additionally, if you're in a city, the cost of doing so can be prohibitive. Getting permits to use ball fields or courts is tough and generating enough interest will take both time and money.

However, you will find quite a few people interested in most areas and if you can find the space to play, starting a league, or just putting together a pickup game every few days or weeks is a great way to meet new people.

School or Classes

If you're already in school, this isn't really an "option", but a necessity. However, if you're interested in meeting people and you're currently out of school or never attended, taking an extension class can be a fantastic way to meet new people and build a collection of new correspondences.

Most community colleges offer a number of adult extensions that are usually very affordable and local. These classes include practical topics like software instruction, accounting and foreign languages, and fun stuff like pottery, music, or dance.

Choose a class based on the type of person you want to meet and the situation you're most comfortable in. The last thing you want is to be out of your element and uncomfortable around new people and therefore unable to talk to them.

Throwing Your Own Events

A lot of you are going to freeze up just reading this, but bear with me.

Eventually, the stuff we've been talking about will start to sink in and you'll develop a strong understanding of what it takes to make people happy and keep them engaged.

When you get to that point, why not throw a party or event at your house? As the host, you control the flow of people, what everyone will do, and what they think of you. Well, maybe not that last one, but you'll definitely feel a lot better about the event if you're in charge of it. People coming to you and introducing themselves makes the process infinitely easier.

You can rightfully put together any event in this chapter on your own, but make sure you have the resources and expertise needed for whatever the event entails. The last thing you want to do is push it too far and create a situation where you're uncomfortable despite all your hard work.

Other Ideas for Events You Can Throw:

For those interested in getting out there and taking control of your social life, here are a few more ideas for events you can throw to draw people to your home.

Old Fashioned BBQ – The classic neighbourhood barbecue is perfect for drawing people to your house. The best part is that you have enough to do to keep you busy and not force you to socialize 100% of the time. Make sure to provide food and drink for all ages and types – including vegetarians and non-drinkers.

Birthday Party – You can throw your own birthday party, or better yet, have a party for someone you're friends with. While the focus of the event will be on the person whose birthday it is, the mere act of having people in your home and showing them around creates an aura of sociability and opens doors for future get-togethers.

Sporting Event – If you're an athlete, get some friends or acquaintances together and go play a sport. You can use craigslist, meetup.com or Facebook to find people who like to play Football, Cricket, Softball, or any other sport that you're a fan of. You'll be surprised how many people are up for a good game.

House Party – A house party is as simple as it gets, but it can also get out of hand quickly, so make sure to put controls in place. Only invite people you know in some way and ask them to limit how many people they bring. Make sure to have plenty of food and drink in place and ask certain people to supplement with their own food and drink too. Also, let your neighbours know you're having a party so they can attend or at least not call the police on you.

Cocktails or Theme Party – On the other end of the "drinking" related party, there is the classic cocktail party. These are great if you are in an older set or know people less likely to attend an informal party. If you have the space, consider themed parties like garden parties, dinners, or pool events.

Pet Event – If you have a pet, this is an incredibly easy way to meet new people. I was often invited to parties with my dog when I was younger, and as a result I met a lot of very interesting people. You don't even need to meet them at home (if you're afraid of 10 dogs running amok in your living room) – a local park or beach is just as perfect.

Work Functions

For the shy, self-conscious individual, nothing is more stressful (except maybe a blind date) than a work function. Being forced or coerced into spending additional time with people you may or may not have any relationship with but have to see day after day, plus your boss, can make for an awkward evening if you're a social wallflower.

It's awkward enough if you develop relationships with people in which you rarely talk and yet see each other constantly. After a certain amount of time, there's an understanding that you just don't talk to each other. So, what happens if you breach that understanding and start up a conversation?

Nothing. Absolutely nothing. Nine times out of ten, the awkwardness you're imagining just doesn't exist. People like to imagine all the horrible, uncomfortable situations they're about to create for themselves, but in reality, nothing of the sort happens when you just act like yourself and interact with other people comfortably.

Conferences and Meetings

When it comes time to present an idea, get in on a call or be a part of a think tank style interaction with your co-workers, you'll need to be likable or your ideas simply won't get across.

The problem, however, is that by the very nature of most workplaces everyone has a different perspective that informs how they see you and how they respond to everything you do.

To manipulate those viewpoints separately is nearly impossible. You must be as generally likable as possible from as many perspectives as possible.

Here's how you'll do that:

Avoid Sarcasm and Jokes – Being funny is one thing, but it needs to be sharp, to the point, and not directed at anyone. You never know when someone in the room might take part of what you say personally. It's not worth making a mistake and making a fool of yourself.

Making a Convincing Argument – Never assume anything about anyone in the room. Just because your immediate boss understands the issue and agrees with you doesn't mean someone else doesn't need further explanation. Cover all details and don't belittle any viewpoints. If you think something's obvious, don't roll your eyes or act like it should be obvious. It could be insulting.

Make Eye Contact and Be Confident – Body language is important in all interactions, but in none more so than at work. If you want people to respect and follow along with what you're saying, you'd better stand straight, look them all in the eyes and generate rapport through your confident demeanour. Look everyone in the eye so that they can see how sure you are of yourself. It will bleed through in their impression of you.

Be Willing to Adapt – If something isn't working, change it up. Mirroring doesn't really work when you're talking to multiple people at the same time, so you really need to be yourself, but sometimes you can make small adjustments and see how they affect the people you are talking to.

Work place interactions are tough. Meetings and presentations can be murder. If you're nervous, don't feel alone. Millions of men and women get up every day and present something to their colleagues, but if you can maintain your calm, outward confidence and develop a strong position in the room, I guarantee those people will like you far more than if you let nerves get the best of you.

Chapter Eleven:

Dating

"Dating should be less about matching outward circumstances than meeting your inner necessity."

From the first paragraph, I told you this book wasn't a dating guide. There are a LOT of very good dating books out there for women. If you want someone to show you how to meet the opposite sex and find a healthy relationship, I can point you in the right direction. But, let's be honest – wanting to be likable is one of the most important steps to being successful in dating. If you want to be successful in a relationship, or even just on a date, you *have to* be likable to the point that the other person cannot help but pursue you. What we've been discussing is not just for meeting new friends or getting people to like you at work – it's a foundational tool to being likable to the opposite sex.

When you're trying to meet a prospective partner, everything in this book is vitally important.

For the most part, I recommend finding a way to meet someone new in a low stress situation, at least until you feel comfortable in places like night clubs and parties (much higher stress levels). However, despite the outward discomfort you may experience, the process is pretty much the same.

The real difference is whether you meet someone cold for the first time or if you meet them through someone else. A date you meet through a friend will already have a good indication of the type of person you are, usually playing up the good parts.

So, your job is to keep those good parts in focus and to provide context for the rest. Talk about your family, the goals you have in life and the ways in which you'll get ahead in life.

Before the Date Even Begins...

Before you even land that date, you need to do your prep work.

I'm not talking about mastering a cheat sheet list of pickup lines, or trying on every outfit in your closet to make a killer first impression. I'm talking about knowing the essentials that will make you an expert on the opposite sex.

There are universal rules to becoming likeable to the opposite sex, and once you know what they are you can decode a person's desire right off the bat.

To some, it's known as their language of love.

Every person is different, and everyone responds to you differently.

However, there are five ways that you can actually activate desire, passion, and lust in others and when you actively pay attention to their love language (which is essentially how they receive love from another), then you can always win at the dating game and become someone that magnetically attracts people to you!

The Five Languages of Love are words of affirmation, acts of service, affection, quality time and gifts.

Words of affirmation can be compliments, pillow talk, or just verbal expression ("You look beautiful in that dress,"). It makes the other person feel valued, special and appreciated.

Acts of service can be anything that your partner does for you, such as put gas in your car (so you don't have to stop at the gas station on your way to work) or arrange for a special date night for the upcoming weekend.

Affection is anything that shows your partner or date you're thinking of him/her. It could be your arm draped around her shoulder, a spontaneous kiss, a hug or being sexually intimate. Affection is any form of a physical act that makes the other person feel loved and accepted by you.

Quality time is the fourth expression of love, which includes any time spent together. Many people need this in their relationship to reconnect emotionally and physically, and to tighten the bond.

It doesn't matter what the activity is—a night out at the movies, a walk in the park, lying in bed together talking about your day, or not even talking at all, but simply being together by cuddling on the couch.

The fifth love language is **gifts**. This is any token to show your thoughtfulness. It could be a bouquet of flowers, a pair of

ticket to see a band play, or a nice dinner out.

Now that you know what the love languages are, you need to assess what your date, or partner's specific love language is.

No two people are alike, and neither are the ways in which they best receive love.

As you go on a date, and get to know your new love interest, (or if you're in a relationship) get to know your significant other or spouse on a deeper level, ask these important questions:

What made you feel loved as a child?

What made ME feel loved as a child?

When you get to know someone, what is one of the first things you like to do for them?

What is one of the first things I like to do for them?

How did your parents show you that they loved you growing up? (did they bring you a small present after you had a bad day? Did they shower you with affection?) Then, ask yourself the same question.

Often, what we experienced as a child in love, we tend to repeat as an adult. So, if you were given affection by a loving parent, you probably crave that same level of affection in your adult relationship. The same goes for gifts, acts of service, or quality time.

The First Date   "What you're supposed to do when you don't like a thing is change it. If you can't change it, change the way you think about it. Don't complain." – Maya Angelou

To start with, go into every first date with a plan in mind. Don't assume you'll be able to just "wing it" and get away with saying whatever you want. Don't give away too much either.

You should stick to safe topics, the same things you would discuss when you meet someone for the first time, but delve a little deeper into the details about your life that will generate deeper rapport in a romantic relationship.

A good first date should take place somewhere open, yet relaxed enough to facilitate conversation.

Make sure you're active as well. If there is a lull in conversation, you both have a viable distraction to keep you engaged in the date. Have fun! Bowling or mini-golf are perfect for a first date.

Dinner and coffee are both good options too, but again, if the conversation lulls, you don't want your date to think you're uninteresting.

Meeting Your Date

When you first meet a new date and you feel a physical attraction to them, a lot of the stuff we've been talking about might just go right out the side of your head in a single flush. Don't worry, that's normal.

The key to successfully meeting a prospective date is to practice a LOT so that you're ready for whatever happens when you get caught in an unexpected situation.

If you go out only once every five months and collapse when you make a mistake, of course you'll have problems. Instead, maintain a smooth, confident approach to meeting new people and you'll be able to generate rapport over time with anyone you meet. It's like riding a bike – eventually it becomes second nature and you forget how freaking hard it was the first time out.

The Role of Alcohol

Bars are one thing, but alcohol comes up in a lot of situations. It's available at most parties and in just about any restaurant you take a date.

Plus, many outings will naturally end up back at a bar. So, what do you do when the option to drink becomes available? Is it good for your social interactions or bad?

Honestly, it depends on you and your attitude toward alcohol. In reality, most of what we attribute to alcohol is just us wanting to be more active and engaging. Alcohol is just a depressant.

It lowers inhibitions and relaxes your body so that the things you want to express come out.

If you're a happy person with lots to say, you'll start babbling to perfect strangers. If you're secretly very upset about something, you may start sharing your anger or annoyance with anyone close enough to listen.

Drinking does very little other than open an outlet to tap into the things you already want to do. It doesn't *make you* more sociable. It just helps you access your social side. At the same time, it also makes you a little sloppy, not very clear, and a heck of a lot less coherent. So, imagine if you could tap into your social side without alcohol – you'd be even better off.

Not Drinking to Stay Into It

Drinking can be a problem for many people. You never really know what emotions it will drum up. Sometimes you might turn into the life of the party while other times you might get sleepy or depressed.

In either case, you're going to put yourself out there the moment you put a drink to your lips and that makes it far harder to control the impression people gain of you.

So, if you decide not to drink in a social situation where alcohol is a part of the interaction, you should be ready for things to become occasionally awkward. People who do drink are a lot less funny when you're sober, but that's not necessarily a big deal if you make the conscious decision not to let it bother you too much.

When to Avoid Alcohol

There are some situations where I deem it necessary to remain sober. These are times when alcohol will clearly put you at a disadvantage in the interaction with other people. Trust me – these are times when you simply need to back up and get a soda instead. The chances for making mistakes or creating an unlikable impression are too high.

Work Functions – Your boss, the people you work next to every day and possibly members of other departments you've never met before all converging in one place. Not only are they the most likely to judge you negatively, they will see you the next day and five days a week every week after that, so stupid things while drinking will make your life a lot harder.

With In Laws or Family – Family is extremely judgmental and for most people their opinion is most important. You not only want to avoid doing anything silly or letting anything slip that you're not supposed to talk about, but you want to be sure that you don't upset anyone with excessive behaviours. It's a lot less funny when your mother-in-law sees you swinging on a chandelier.

Holidays – This is up for interpretation, but drinking on the holidays can make a lot of things more complicated. Usually there is a lot of travel and logistical decisions involved in visiting people, buying gifts and making dinner. If you're drunk, all of those things are much harder to control.

On Planes or Trains – Imagine being stuck for five or six hours next to a stranger who is drunk and not very courteous in regards to your personal space. Now imagine you're the drunk person.

Drinking on a plane or train may take the edge off, but it can also ruin a perfectly good opportunity to meet a stranger if you get carried away with the mini-bottles.

On a Date – Drinking on a date is almost always a big no-no. Not only does it make a negative impression on your date, it can lead to you saying things you'd rather not. To top it off, having sex on an early date doesn't necessarily have to be a bad thing, but if it happens when you're drinking, it can ruin a perfectly good early relationship.

In Public – Obviously, drinking in public can have bad side effects. The last thing you want to do is to make a fool of yourself when there are random strangers around you. If you're going to drink, make sure you're inside or at least in a controlled environment.

This is just a partial list too. Really, you should just use your best judgment. The test I use is whether or not I can comfortably exit a situation without it causing any problems. An airplane, a work party, and a date are all situations you can't just get up and walk away from. So, you should stay sober to make sure you don't overdo things.

Leaving a Lasting Impression on Those You Meet It's all fine and good to be likeable and for someone to actively enjoy spending time talking to you, but what happens the next day or two or three days after that. If you run into that same person on the street in a week, will they remember you?

Will they instantly start laughing and flapping their arms in reference to inside joke you shared with them?

Part of interacting with other people is learning how to leave a powerful, lasting impression on them. Whether you're on a date, in a business meeting or on a job interview, the other person needs to form a permanent, lasting impression of who you are and why they like you.

If the first splash you make in someone's mind is a big one, you're sure to stick around. Of course, a big first impression must also be a good first impression to be effective, so don't go in spouting expletives or walking on your hands to get attention.

According to a study conducted by psychologists at Sonoma State University and the University of Texas at Austin in the United States, one of the strongest indicators of a first impression is appearance.

People instantly judge you based on how you look. And in a lot of cases, the judgment is accurate. There are a few reasons for this. If you dress poorly and don't take care of yourself, you probably don't have a lot of confidence and the image of an introvert will likely prove to be accurate.

If you dress well and are clean shaven with a slick haircut, you project an image of confidence and you will work to fulfil that image. Here are some specific things found to affect the first impression of someone:

Smile - A full, bright smile is item number one on the positive impression checklist. By smiling when you meet someone you invite them to get to know you and show that you are a positive person interested in developing a relationship.

Posture - How you stand can have a big impression on someone as well. For example, your posture can basically tell someone how tired you are, how confident you are among other people and whether you are eager to meet and get to know them.

Dress - Clean, neat dressers are those who have their lives together and know what they want. Those who don't change clothes or wear baggy clothes to hide themselves in are not comfortable in their own skin and it shows.

Tension - Tension can be relayed in a number of ways. How often you move, the way you stand, how quickly you respond to questions, and more. Stress and tension, either because of meeting someone new or due to an outside factor can instantly make you appear less interesting and can force someone away before they can make a lasting impression.

Energy - This works in degrees. Too little energy and you appear distant and disinterested. Too much, however, and you are borderline confrontational and overwhelming. Be energetic and excited to meet someone without making them feel uncomfortable.

Distinction - Stand out in your own personal way. Find ways to dress differently from people in your situations or to be more interesting in subtler ways, such as telling funny stories or inviting people into conversations actively. You don't need a "thing" but if you have one, by all means, use it to distinguish yourself from others.

It's easy to stand out if you are confident, well-groomed and interesting. Don't let yourself define these things by social convention, however. Be yourself and work within your expanded comfort zone to build new relationships and make a powerful, lasting first impression.

Be Fantastically Fascinating! (It's really, really easy.) If you want to be more likeable, and despite your desire to stand out from the crowd, you may still wonder (especially in a romantic capacity), how do I actually become unique, and captivating? Here's some simple tips to getting there, today—and capture the eyes of admirers, everywhere:

The subtle attraction technique. The subtle attraction technique is one of my favorite techniques in this whole book because it automatically brings people towards you, without you having to put on a show, buy an entire wardrobe or spend hundreds of dollars on gifts-with the mere hope they'll change their attitude about you.

The subtle attraction technique is about harnessing that little self-defeating voice in your head that tells you you're not good enough, smart enough or attractive enough, and beating it to a pulp.

The whole idea behind this technique is that every single one of us have something that drives us. But, if we aren't as successful financially or social popular as we'd like (or if our relationship/dating life isn't what we want it to be), than what is perhaps driving us, isn't positive but negative.

If you aren't getting what you want in life, it's because your thoughts may be negative, and they are driving you from taking more changes in love and beyond. All you have to do to change everything in your life around is by changing how you view yourself around.

This technique is all about changing the dialog going on inside your head, and you can easily do that by turning each negative thought into its positive opposite.

So, if you think, "I'm not attractive enough to be with that person," immediately think the positive opposite, "I'm attractive enough to be with that person!" Take about ten seconds to feel it.

Feel it in your bones, and your soul. Believe it with all your might, and repeat this exercise any time someone or something triggers your insecurity. Positivity is attractive, and draws people to you. Simply by focusing on positive thoughts, you have the power to magnetize yourself easily, effortlessly and immediately!

The fascination volcano technique. Do you remember that movie, Ferris Bueller? His teacher in the movie spoke in a monotone voice—no fluctuation in tone, and no excitement. As he spoke, he (hilariously) put the students to sleep—so much that one student was drooling on his table!

While the actor did an incredible job playing the role of the most boring man on Earth, he also clearly demonstrated what repels people away. He wasn't fascinating at all, but boring, unenthused, and without a spark of passion in his life. There was nothing about him that attracted others.

When you want to magnetize more people to you, you have to think like them: does the way you speak bring others in, or have them turning around and walking away in search of a more dynamic person to listen to?

To apply the fascination volcano technique, it's simple. All you have to do is focus on your tone.

If you want someone else to be excited in what you're saying, fluctuate your tone. Sound excited about what you're talking about and others will be too! If you're on a date, you can even start your story by laughing about something for a quick second, and then smiling, lead in with the story your date will laugh at too. Speak in a moderate volume, so that they can hear you clearly.

Pause for dramatic effect (just for a second!) and let them chime in on the story, too. Being dynamic is about the dialog between the two of you. Tell stories that are relevant, set up your story to promote a sense of intrigue from your audience (or date, significant other, etc.) and react to their reaction!

The Engagement technique that work on anyone, anywhere. The engagement technique is all about making others feel good.

If you think about it, we are all selfish—focusing on what our personal desires, needs, and wants really are.

Whether you get nervous in a new environment, or you simply want to make a better impression on a date, the engagement technique (through applying the art of a compliment) is the perfect way to become well liked, popular and best of all, magnetizing.

Engage others—your spouse, a significant other, or simply anyone you want to impress. Practice it on strangers to gain confidence, and then apply it on someone that you really want to impress!

- "That color looks incredible on you."
- "You helped me so much, thank you!"
- You make me feel beautiful/gorgeous/etc."
- "I love how you make it feel."

- "(Their name), you're so funny, fun to be around, etc." (By the way, an additional way to make people feel even more special is by starting a compliment by saying their name. For whatever reason, people love to hear the sound of their name, and it makes them feel special. After all, you're not spitting out this compliment to everyone you see. It's unique to them, and saying their name is the perfect way to reaffirm that.) Remember, being likeable is about projecting kindness, positivity, a caring nature; fun loving nature, confidence and empathy. The techniques you just read about will do just that (and much, much more!)

Whether you're single or you've been married for the last ten years, you've wondered from time to time how to enhance the romance, bring on more pleasure, or simply how to tighten the bond.

Even if you're in the relationship of your dreams, you're not immune to the 'ebb and flow', the ups and downs that every relationship goes through—but when you apply love, trust, great communication and strive for a relationship worth having—the 'ebb and flow' only solidifies your connection.

No matter what you may be going through right now in your relationship (whether you're single and looking for 'the one', have recently met him/her, or have been with the same person for years), these five sensual love building triggers are your golden ticket to everlasting bliss, romance and passion.

The 'Give' Approach

Isn't it funny how at the beginning of a new relationship—right when our desire for the other person is at an all-time high—we go to the ends of the Earth to make them happy?

But, as time goes on, we start complaining more, and doing less. We do the dishes or cook less, as we nag at them about this or that, more.

The problem is, the other person hasn't changed—we have. We focus on what we're not getting, or getting less of than we used to—

and whether we realize it or not, we begin to make a mental checklist of all that our partner is doing wrong, instead of focusing on what our partner is doing right.

Ultimately, what that leads to is a 'take' approach, isn't of a giving one. Do you want to bring more amazing things to your relationship? Are you complaining about not getting the romance you used to? Then give more.

When you come from a place of giving – which refocuses your attention to a love state— then you have the power to transform your entire energy, and entire relationship.

Focus on giving. Think about your partner every single day. Don't think about what your partner has done for you, but what you can do for your partner. An oil change? A hot meal on the table? A compliment? It doesn't have to be big, but it does have to be sincere.

When you come from a place where you're giving, you're full of love, gratitude and joy about the person you're with—which is what will exponentially increase the romance, the love, the appreciation and passion in your relationship. It will allow you to turn on your secret auto-magnetism without even realizing it!

Know Your Partner's Body Language

Being able to decode body language is a powerful relationship tool. It can allow you to bypass potential arguments, shift your energy (so you can come from a place of love, not complaints) and demonstrate compassion to him—sometimes, without saying a thing.

When you can read your partner's body language, you can easily tap into what they need from you, and how you can best give it to them. For example, if your partner crosses their arms when upset, then you can adjust your behaviour to fit their needs or desires. If your partner smiles every time they asks you if its ok if they stays out late with their friends tomorrow night for happy hour, then you know it's something they're really excited about— which can clue you into their feelings.

You can then adjust your expectations, and be in a position to understand what they want (something that he will be very appreciate about.)

You have more power than you realize to make your partner happy and bring forth a whole level of attraction to the forefront—so why not tap into your partner's body language, in order to enhance the passion, love and happiness you two feel when together?

Pay attention to their body language, and focus on their happiness. When you do, they'll be eager to return the favour.

Know Your Partner's Sex Language

Have you ever noticed how affectionate couples become after a night of really passionate sex?

Sex is responsible for activating oxytocin, otherwise known as the 'cuddle hormone'—and while men may have the reputation for having sex on the brain more than females, the act of sex is equally important for both sexes.

Think of sex as the ultimate physical expression of your love, devotion and connection to your partner. You may think, "I already know that," but what you may not know is how fundamentally important it is to know how to give your partner what they want, in the way that they want and need it.

Everyone has a different sexual style. Yours may be more passionate than your partners, or you might like a more experimental angle than your partner does. Try thinking about their sexual needs.

Do they go crazy when you tease a little bit before letting them touch you? Do they enjoy the build-up, or being taken ravenously right away?

When you focus on how sex makes them feel, then you can give them a pleasure they've never experienced before.

Take your time. Tease, play and seduce your partner by hitting their erogenous zones (those pleasurable, extra sensitive spots on their body), working your angle from head to toe.

When you practice catering to their sex language, their ability to show you more love, attention, devotion and romance will go to a whole new level.

Bring on More Face to Face

If you've ever wondered how to bring a greater sense of connection to your relationship (or perhaps you've recently tried everything you can think of to ignite the passion) face-to-face time is key.

It's a perfect little technique for sparking the connection that the two of you used to feel, but thanks to your busy lives, haven't made a priority. All you have to do in order to make this technique work is set aside about twenty minutes, and turn off all distractions.

If you have kids, do this on a night where you've hired a babysitter. If your phone and other technological devises are normally on, turn them off. When you do the face-to-face technique, nothing is more important than you and your partner.

The key to this exercise is allowing the two of you to be together, without anything else getting in your way. All you have to do is sit across from one another (sit with your legs crossed on the floor) and hold each other's hands. Your knees can touch, but nothing else. Don't kiss. Don't talk. Just look at one another for as long as you can (up to 20 minutes).

Now, the first few times you do this exercise, looking at one another may feel awkward, or uncomfortable even. You don't have to be comfortable with it—you can even laugh if the exercise makes you laugh. The whole point is to learn how to feel connected once again, and this exercise makes it easy.

The eyes are the pathway for the soul, and if you have long abandoned the habit of looking your partner in the eyes when speaking to him, this technique will be a deeply powerful exercise you'll want to continue bringing into your relationship.

What Can I Do For You?

Be honest—when was the last time you asked your partner, "What can I do for you?" If you can't remember, it's been too long. This sensual love building trigger is one of the most powerful exercises of all because it allows you to form a deep emotional connection—simply by communicating how you feel with one, simple question.

"What can I do for you?" It may be that your partner wants to cuddle on the couch, or have wild, passionate sex, or just eat a meal together without interruption and talk about their day. It doesn't matter what they might want. Remember, this exercise is about communicating your love, so that your partner will feel so insanely drawn to you (thanks to your magnetizing likeability) that you'll ultimately get what YOU want from the relationship. Imagine getting a greater sense of connection from your partner.

Imagine getting a harmonious home life, free of nit picking and disagreements. This one, powerful question of "What can I do for you?" will make them feel loved, honoured, and respected. It's a powerful, but simple exercise I believe in, because I've seen it give me the results I want, time and time again.

When you combine the five sensual love building triggers with this explosive *pleasure center intensifier* technique, your love life will become something that others only dream of.

Now, this one is perfect when the flame of passion has begun to dwindle in your relationship, or if after several disagreements with your significant other, you want to mend the disconnection.

This technique may seem physical, but it's actually all about repairing or tightening the emotional connection, through the physical act.

The *pleasure center intensifier* technique is all about focusing on your partner's erogenous zones to enhance passion, bliss and longing and when done correctly, it's a shortcut to bringing the relationship back to where it was in the honeymoon stage!

All you have to do is touch your partner in his erogenous zones—those pleasure point and sensitive areas of your partner's body. Lightly trace their toes, bottom of the feet, stomach, back of the legs, earlobes, neck, lips, and back.

Then, after taking time with this (by stroking, rubbing and tracing the body), you can let them ravish you. It's powerful, and the passion is immediate!

How to Merit and Maintain Others' Trust

Trust is a point of contention for many individuals. Earning it is exceptionally hard and losing it only takes a few moments, but once you have it and if you can hold it, you will create lasting friendships and relationships that can fundamentally alter your life.

So, it's incredibly important that you learn not only what it takes to merit trust from others but how to gain and hold that trust.

First, consider what people expect from each other. Putting cynicism aside, most people expect nothing more than honesty from their friends and loved ones. If you want someone to trust you, give them every reason to do so.

More than that, don't let situations develop in which you don't appear to be honest. For example, neglecting to inform someone about something that they need to know or feel they need to know could be seen as a breach of trust.

Just because you don't tell your girlfriend that you are going to Las Vegas for the weekend doesn't mean she won't feel hurt if she finds out, even if nothing happens. You create a situation where there might not have been one.

This type of situation can occur in almost any setting - in a workplace where you neglect to inform your boss that you are running behind on a project, a family function you make an excuse to miss or a friend you leave out of an outing with other friends, simply by omission.

Beyond honesty, trust is built on a sense that you and the other person would mutually sacrifice anything to help each other. That means you need to lose any selfish tendencies.

For example, in conversation, when someone starts to tell you about their problems or even just their day, be careful not to interrupt, change the subject or go into "me too" mode.

These responses can instantly shut down the other person and force them to hold back the things they want to tell you. Moreover, they won't grow to trust you with the details of their life.

Sometimes listening is more powerful than anything you can do for someone. You don't need to proffer solutions or tell someone about how you went through a similar trial in your life. You just need to listen and be there for them as a friend or loved one.

Trust forms the foundation of all relationships - don't treat it lightly. Once you generate trust with someone you care about, do everything your power to maintain that trust by being honest, showing you care and being selfless in your role as friend or loved one.

Tips for Building and Maintaining Trust

Always Direct Criticism Toward Someone – If you have a problem with someone, direct your criticism toward them. Don't discuss their issues behind their back or avoid discussing it. Even if it is an attempt to spare their feelings it can generate feelings of distrust. Be upfront and clear with everything you need to tell them.

Avoid Gossip and Rumors – Don't gossip about people you know, hold secrets or talk about others behind their backs. If it gets out, it can be a serious blow to the trust you've developed with them.

No Exclusions for How You Treat People – Don't treat one friend or co-worker different from how you treat another. You may like someone more, but if you consciously treat them differently, It will create a divide among you, especially with friends or coworkers.

Provide Equal Attention – Provide equal attention to everyone in a group. This goes double for employees or coworkers who can misinterpret the imbalance of as them being pushed out of the decision making process.

Conflict Resolution – If there is a conflict, resolve it like an adult. Discuss the problem, don't be confrontational or point fingers. Be willing to accept blame but also ask questions so both parties know where they stand. This goes for all conflicts – from your love life to your friends. When it comes to developing and maintaining trust, you need to be honest in every way. Intentions are not enough – you need to show that you consider their feelings and concerns before you act or speak. Do this and you will become a trustworthy friend for many people.

Exercises and Questions This chapter, I want to keep things simple. I don't have any specific exercises for you. Instead, I want you to record the last time you did any of the things in this chapter and what the result was. Now, work toward finding new opportunities to throw yourself into those situations.

Situation	Result
Party	
Bar	
Meetup Group or Club	
Internet	
Sporting Event or League	
School or Class	
Events at Your Home	
Work Functions	
Date	

Now, I want you to make a commitment to attempt at least one of each of these in the next 6 weeks. Record the results in a separate notebook so that you can follow exactly how you perform. Note: things like dating should be done more than once every 6 weeks or so. Aim to interact with people as often as possible, not just when a book tells you to.

Chapter Twelve:

How to Make Friends and Keep Them

"Life isn't about finding yourself. Life is about creating yourself."

— George Bernard Shaw

Being nice to people is one thing, but what about making friends and keeping them after the initial conversation?

How do you stand out so much that someone will want to know you for the foreseeable future and better yet, spend time with you?

There are a lot of factors at work here. People are not selfish by nature, but they also have only so much time in the day and need to know that when they spend time with someone it will not be a drain on their resources. What do you bring to a friendship that will encourage a long term relationship?

All these factors, when combined, will make up a lot of how you approach the people you meet and how you generate interest from a new friend or better yet, romantic interest.

Being Confident

Confidence is the cornerstone of friendship. Not only do you need to bring a strong, powerful personality to your interactions with any new friend, you need to show them that you won't be the clingy, needy person that so many people fear.

If you put a drain on their financial or emotional resources, eventually they'll ask "why am I friends with this person?" You'll stress them out – and no one wants a friend like that.

Don't Worry about Making Them Happy

Part of confidence is being so sure of yourself that you don't feel the urge to make someone else happy all the time.

Stop worrying that what you say will upset someone. If it's really what you feel and it's not outright rude or mean (see chapter 2), let it fly and if they're really your friends, they'll appreciate your opinion.

Too many times, people with self-esteem issues will hold back their opinions, waiting for someone else to confirm it, then agree with them. I'm sure you've done it. You really want to see an action movie, but feel a little unsure because you're embarrassed by how cheesy it is.

So, instead of just saying, "Let's go see Battle Explosion IV", you ask, "What do you want to see?" and hope they agree with your opinion.

The problem with this approach is that you expend a huge amount of energy trying to make other people happy. You worry about what they want and what they'll think of your opinions.

Stop doing that. Be honest and forthright. So what if the other people in your group don't agree with you? You're still a good person who's perfectly likable. They might decide to give that movie a shot, just because you recommended it and you'll then get a chance to open their mind to a new genre.

Don't Be Afraid to Upset Others

Things can get tricky here, because the last thing you want to do is actively upset someone who you consider your friend. But, at the same time, it's silly to hold back your opinion when you're afraid it could hurt someone else's feelings.

This is the exact reason why so many people are unfit to be in charge. They worry constantly that what they say will put out their employees or subordinates and that it will ruin their friendship. The result, though, is awkwardness that further strains the relationship.

While you may not run an Office somewhere, the idea is the same. You cannot go around avoiding the tough topics.

If someone upsets you, let them know. If someone shouldn't be driving because they've had too many drinks, take their keys away.

If they look goofy in a certain outfit, say something – it's what friends do. Just go back to chapter two and make sure you do it in a friendly way.

Honesty and bluntness are not the same thing, and the line between them can cause rifts in your likability, so be wary of how what you say affects your friends.

Dump the Bad Influences

If you have someone in your life that causes you to feel upset, angry or simply stressed all the time distance yourself from that person.

Being likable is one thing, but allowing someone to harm how you view the world because you're unsure of what it will do to them if you end the friendship is unwise. It only hurts you and will draw away too much of the energy you've put into becoming likable in the first place.

Handling Criticism

"Often those that criticise others reveal what he himself lacks."

— Shannon L. Alder

Criticism is tricky. It's painful to hear, but it can also be incredibly valuable when you work toward improving yourself.

If someone tells you honestly that you make jokes at other people's expense when drinking, maybe you should take that as a cue to stop drinking when you go out, instead of taking it personally and getting angry at a friend who is only trying to help you.

Take What Other People Say to You in Stride

Some people are out to get you, but not many and most of the time, even they privately just want to help you out a bit.

So, when you receive a comment on your behaviour or an opinion of your judgment, take it all in stride and be willing to adjust so you can fix whatever has been pointed out. It is hard, I know, but it is also extremely helpful for you when trying to be more likable.

Develop Common Responses to Criticism

A good way to handle criticism is to start categorizing it and develop common responses that will work in any situation.

For example, if someone told you that you were a loud chewer, instead of saying "who cares", you could say, "I didn't realize, thanks for the heads up."

It's not rude, and it's not self-degrading. It just recognizes the criticism, shows that you're taking it into consideration and that you will work toward fixing the problem.

See the Good and Filter Out the Bad

Of course, with all that said, I don't want you to start taking every criticism you hear and try to fix what's "wrong" with you.

There's nothing wrong with you and if someone tries to say otherwise, they're not helping. The goal of this exercise is not to hurt your feelings, but to learn to see yourself from someone else's perspective.

It's not easy to do, but it can have a profound effect on your outlook of the world. So, to make sure you get the most out of the criticism you receive, we need to set up a filtration system that pulls out the bad stuff and sets it aside.

Some people are just jerks – they will say things that are not constructive and that are aimed at hurting you more than at helping you.

If you can recognize those moments and make changes that take advantage of the good without considering the bad, you'll be far better off.

Avoiding Manipulation

One of the biggest risks in "trying" to be likable is that others will try to take advantage of your friendliness.

There are always going to be people out there who willingly partake of your generosity and as a result, overstay their welcome in your life.

The same as you must learn to be friendly under any circumstances, you should learn how to identify manipulative behaviour and say "No" when it is necessary.

Saying no while remaining friendly is easier said than done though. It requires an internal test that tells you when something goes too far and you need to "change" the interaction. Need some help? Here are some tips:

1. Determine the Motivation behind Someone's Statement – First up, determine if someone is honestly trying to take advantage of you or if they are simply asking for help. There are a few factors here:

Do they ask for help often? Do they offer anything in return? Do they ask or assume? How do they respond to a no? Do you actually want to help them?

In my hand will gladly provide you with some kind of recompense.

experience, people who want your help and are simply looking for a friendly

You can say no, of course, but they will understand that they are extracting value from you and that it requires some form of reciprocation.

Now, flip that on its head and look at what a manipulative friend will do.

They will *assume* you're going to help them. They think of their friends as tools just as they do their possessions.

2. Analyse How it Affects Your Life – If you are not sure of the motivation behind a request or if you're leaning toward it being manipulative, ask yourself how the request directly affects your life.

Is it going to cost you money, time, or pain and suffering?

Or is it an easy thing you can do between work and home that won't cost you a dime.

Sometimes, even if someone is being manipulative and making assumptions, it doesn't put you out at all.

The real key is in knowing how to draw the line between these moments and those in number four.

Make a Decision about How to Respond – Decide what you'll do. If you know the request won't put you out at all or if you're willing to help this friend because they honestly need your help and recognize what you're doing to offer it, go for it.

But, if you feel that you're being taken advantage of and you really don't want to do it, be ready to respond with a "no".

Draw a Line for When You Will Stop Responding – For situations that fall into number two where you feel someone is taking you for granted but it really doesn't put you out that much, learn to draw lines that can be enforced for future requests.

For example, if someone gets a ride home from work with you every day and never really asks or offers gas money, the impact on your life is minimal.

But, if they start asking you to stop at the grocery store first or to provide them some spare cash, know that it's time to draw the line.

Tell them that you're happy to drive them home but they'll need to pay for gas or find time when you're not as busy. Or just say no. The goal here is not to be rude or to say no for the sake of saying no. It's to protect yourself against people who see your likability and assume it means you're a pushover.

Remember back to how your parents responded to questions like that – would they say yes or no and what would their reasoning be in both cases?

Being in Control of Your Own Actions

You're an adult and that means you have the power to make your own decisions, back them up with your emotions and experiences, and use them to assert your position in a relationship.

If someone expects you to do something because you're a nice person, maybe it's time to lay down the law. And, if you do decide to help someone, recognize that you never 'have to' do anything.

Going broke helping a friend with their own bills is not an excuse not to pay your rent. You need to make decisions that ensure you are taken care of first.

If you decide to pour every remaining ounce of your resources into helping other people, so be it, but don't sacrifice yourself to do so. It doesn't generate respect from other people and it surely doesn't make you any more likable – it just makes you "useful".

What People Really Expect of You

Any number of people will go into a new conversation or relationship with expectations. It's normal. But, what's not normal is making assumptions about what someone expects of you. It's an unhealthy way to approach any interaction and can have a negative impact on how other people view you.

Stop Interpreting Intentions – The urge to interpret what you see in someone else's actions is almost built into us as human beings. But, no matter how much a part of your world view it may feel, stop doing it. It will take time to make this change – after all, you've been doing it since your first social interactions in preschool. But, here's a trick that will help you out. When someone does something, instead of asking "why", tell yourself that there is no reason. Imagine that the action magically happened of its own accord, without anyone to blame or link to it, the same as the rain storm the other night or the sunshine last weekend. Sure, there were intentions, but by pretending nothing caused it, you'll be able to get some distance and give them the benefit of the doubt.

Ask Nicely – If you really feel unsure about what someone is doing or asking of you, simply ask them what the point is. This is a pretty simple way to get past all of it. You can use your active listening tactics as well – if someone says something that sounds rude, offer your interpretation and then wait for clarification. These actions will all allow you to generate real impressions without creating any disagreements between each other.

Expect the Best from Others – At the end of the day, no matter how many times you've been burned and how many people seem to be trying to take advantage of your nicer qualities, I implore you to expect the best out of them. Just imagine what happens when you're wrong about someone's so called bad intentions. More often than not, it could be a misunderstanding.

I know the last few sections probably seem contradictory to each other. I tell you to take criticism, then avoid manipulation and then to give everyone the benefit of the doubt. In reality, it's very hard to make the judgment call between all of these different world views.

You're going to have situations where it's very hard to tell whether someone is taking advantage of you or being rude or simply behaving in a different way than you're used to. That's why we wait and see.

Instead of jumping on someone for their outrageous behaviour (and acting a little outrageous ourselves), we wait and determine if anything really merits that kind of anger. More often than not, it doesn't.

Empathy 101

One of the most important aspects of any relationship is empathy. You cannot just interact with someone and listen to their problems – you must go the extra mile and actually feel for them.

It's a tough road that requires a substantial emotional investment, but it works wonders when building a relationship in which you hope to have a healthy back and forth. I've already discussed empathy and why it's such a vital aspect in a likable person, but what about in action – as part of a real world relationship. How does it work then?

Visualizing the Shoe Switch

I'm sure you've heard the age old adage, "Walk a mile in someone else's shoes". Part of a successful interaction with a new friend is to do this on a repeated basis. It can be mentally exhausting at first as you consciously look inside yourself to understand how you'd react to a situation your friend is dealing with, but as you get the hang of it, you'll see that your brains starts to do it automatically.

Imagine your best friend just got in a car accident. Your immediate response is concern.

You want to know if they're okay. Upon hearing they're okay, you relax and turn back to your own concerns, but for your friend, the problems are just starting. Their car is totalled, the other driver is uninsured, they cannot get to work and they could lose her job if the insurance isn't processed fast enough.

Your immediate reaction is "oh good, they're safe," but if you put yourself in their shoes, you'd realize that there is so much more going on under the surface – details that will have just as profound of an impact on their life as a major injury could have.

So, instead of moving on and leaving them to their own problems, you show empathy by driving them to and from work until their check comes in and making sure they have everything they needs.

That's a good friend – not just because you've done something for them, but because you imagined what would happen if you were stuck in the same boat and offered the same support you would want.

The opportunities to step into the skin of someone you love and imagine what would happen in their shoes are numerous.

Life is constantly throwing curveballs in our direction, forcing us to adjust and adapt to what happens.

Having a caring friend or loved one nearby who not only understand but can act to help us cope is a life preserver that anyone would hope for and one that will make you a good friend for life, no matter what kind of relationship you have otherwise.

Provide Value

Back in the Introduction, I talked to you a bit about how Psychologists look at social interactions. They have different theories and while I'm not a licensed psychiatrist (nor have I studied the topic academically), I tend to agree with some theories more than others.

One in particular, social exchange theory, is a very interesting peek into how people interact with each other. It doesn't necessarily represent the full spectrum of people or how they interact with one another, but it does posit an interesting idea about what we expect and what we give in a relationship.

In short, you only stick in a relationship as long as you feel you're getting an equivalent return on your investment.

It's a sterile way to describe an emotional interaction, but it's not far from the mark. After all, how many times have you heard your friends breaking up with their partner because they just "weren't all there"?

If you take and take and never give in return, people will eventually see you as a leech in the friendship and will leave you to find another host.

So, at least part of your relationships needs to be focused on providing value to people you care about. What can you do for them that will show them you're a caring, interested person?

Willingly Admit Your Mistakes

You make mistakes.

You're not alone though – everyone makes mistakes in life. It's those who make changes after a mistake and openly admit what they did wrong who improve and become better people because of them.

In any relationship, the ability to both acknowledge and take responsibility for a mistake will make the difference when it comes to the viability of your relationship.

Don't make excuses, lie, or cover up what you did. Admit it, apologize if it's necessary and learn from what went wrong (so that you don't have to repeat your mistake, again.)

I look at my own mistakes as gifts. Sometimes the gift is a little messier and more painful than I'd like, but it's still a gift, because it gives me an opportunity to fundamentally change part of myself and adjust my worldview so that I never again make that mistake.

Imagine the opportunity to thoroughly adjust your life choices and make a decision that will adapt how you think and live.

Share Time and Energy with Others

Selfishness gets you nowhere. The value I mentioned will come across in the generosity of your friendship. If you're the type of friend who only gives to people who have given to you, you'll develop a relationship as someone who is difficult and selfish.

However, if you focus your energy into giving to anyone who needs your help and openly providing insights and time to those who need it, you'll not only make lots of friends, you'll retain them.

This goes hand in hand with avoiding manipulation and providing value. You need to hit a happy medium where the men and women who you meet can see a powerful personality with a lot to offer that isn't going to let them take advantage.

It's a hard line to walk, but if you maintain your confidence and work at displaying empathy to those around you, it will grow much easier over time.

Exercises and Questions

1. Write down the last time you upset someone. Was it justified or not?

2. Make a list of friends you spend at least 2 hours per week with. How do you spend your time? How willing are you to find new friends?

3. Ask a friend or family member to provide criticism on three areas of your choice. Examples include: love life, how you talk, your health, your activity level, your hobbies.

4. Now, dissect that criticism and look for things that you can take action on now without changing your core personality. Don't get upset. Just set aside anything that isn't practical or constructive.

5. Write down the last five mistakes you made in life and the steps you made to amend and fix those problems. Were you successful?

6. Brainstorm three ways you can give your time to the people you care about and how that time can be used productively to create closer relationships.

Chapter Thirteen:

Putting it all to Good Use

"It is never too late to be what you might have been."

— George Eliot

All the tips in the world are useless if you don't apply them, step by step... ...in order to find someone who you can connect with, share your new values and ideals with and become friends or something more. x It's a hard road to walk, but it gets easier.

The more you practice the exercises, tips and techniques found in this book, the more comfortable and confident you will become!

You'll quickly find that, with a personality like yours, people will come to you. No longer will you need to go out and meet people or seek out dates. They'll see your smooth confidence and radiating energy and will gravitate towards you.

Dating

"You know you're in love when you can't fall asleep because reality is finally better than your dreams."

— Dr. Seuss

Dating, especially when you're still working to develop your self-esteem and become likable to new people, is hard – but it won't always be.

220

Starting from the moment you say 'how are you doing' and at every milestone along the way, you'll be stressed about doing the right or wrong thing, making a fool of yourself, or wasting your time on someone who is not interested in you.

So, how do you take everything we've discussed and create the perfect, streamlined approach to a romantic relationship?

It starts way back in Chapter one when I told you how to be friendly and likable. You need to be relaxed and show that you are the attractive person that your potential partner has been looking for.

You need to show respect, and become knowledgeable about how they best receive and give love. And, you need to come from a giving mind set, so that you can cultivate an ongoing attraction with the one you care for.

Initial attraction is easy, but to become likeable, desired and pursued by your partner for months, years and up to a lifetime, apply the following tips—and watch your love life take off into something you've never experienced before:

Tell it like it is. After taking a workshop on success in relationships by a handful of my greatest relationship idols, I began implementing one of the easiest tools for communication I learned there.

It's called, *what do you want to share?*

What do you want to share is about creating a space for you and your partner to express honesty about anything—and to allow each other to be as bluntly honest as possible.

The basis behind this exercise is this: any time a miscommunication arises in a relationship (even when it gets worked out) there are hidden issues and resentments that lurk beneath the surface.

Sometimes, when people hide what they are really feeling (or only tell the half-truth about what they are feeling), resentments can build and end up manifesting in all aspects of the relationship.

Learning to get into the practice of telling the truth—even when you don't want to because it feels uncomfortable—is a great gift you can give you partner, and yourself.

Instead of being a 'yes man' (or 'yes woman') begin sharing what you feel, what you think and what you know to be true with your partner.

Don't worry about hurting someone else's feelings (just be sure to use "I" statements so you speak from your own experience, instead of blaming your partner for what happened).

In order to do this and be effective with the honest approach, start by picking a time that you and your partner can be alone—no distractions, no prior commitments.

Start the conversation by stating the problem. What was it that upset you, that confused you, or that angered you?

After you describe the details (what happened, how you perceived it to happen, what emotions it stirred up in you), ask your partner for their take on it. How did they perceive it to go?

Work together to come up with a solution. Saying something like, "Do you have any ideas about what we can do to resolve this?" is direct and to the point, and allows you to come from a positive place (which they won't be likely to dismiss).

Avoid the ping-pong game in love. When you're in a relationship—even when things are going well (both people are showing each other love, appreciation and respect) there's room for emotional static to take place.

> *Friction can arise and when it does (before it escalates to the point of an eruptive fight), it's so important to create a safe, comforting space to talk about whatever needs to be said.*

Studies show that the happiest couples do damage control before there's damage to really control.

Meaning, they don't wait for a blow up to occur AND THEN talk about it.

They nip conflict in the bud by proactively having a heart-to-heart discussion quickly and swifty. You can do this while enjoying a meal together, and by placing your hand on your partner's knee or hand.

This can even be done in a work setting, when you need to address a co-worker or manager.

Even if there isn't a conflict that's arisen, you can speak openly to one another during weekly meetings ("heart to heart time!") in order to foster a greater bond and/or sense of community.

The rules are simple: whoever wants the opportunity to talk without interruption, holds onto a heart shaped stone, etc.

They get to talk for five minutes without anyone else chiming in, or offering their perspective or input. Until your discussion is complete, everyone stays put until you've come to a solution together.

No matter what relationship you want to improve, the heart to heart talk is a radical way to change how you communicate, express understanding and promote a greater sense of connection.

Key Points:

In dating, certain things will make the difference in success rates far more so than others.

Here's a cheat sheet of sorts for what to focus your energies on in this book if you're looking for a future partner:

Learn how to listen—be an active listener, and an engaged participant. This means that when someone is talking to you (that you're excited to get to know!) pay attention. Focus on what they're saying. What is he/she excited about?

What is he/she passionate about? What is her work life like?

What is his family like?

Nod and smile to let that person know you're actively listening and interested in what they have to say!

Empathy in action—become involved in what someone else has gone through. Someone that is likeable to the opposite sex is someone who extends himself, and thinks outside of himself. You can demonstrate to others that you feel deeply by nonverbal cues: smiling when they tell you something good, or having a serious expression when they tell you something traumatic that's happen to them communicates a level of trust and connection. Make strong eye contact when they speak or when you speak to them, nod to show sympathy and mimic their body language to suggest understanding.

Confidence and surety of yourself—model your self-assurance by sitting up straight, smiling, and showing off your best self. People are instantly drawn to happy, positive people. When you act like you've got nothing to hide (you're an open book!) and you genuinely love your life, others will want to become part of that. When you focus on staying true to yourself, remind yourself of how you awesome you are, and focus on the new, brave steps you're taking out of your comfort zone, you'll find that life might take you places you used to only dream of going. Enjoy the process. Live it up, date by date!

Work Relationships

Moving beyond dating, the second most stressful form of interaction is with the people you work with.

These are men and women you have to see every single day, regardless of how you get along.

Your family is the same, but with them at least there is an underlying love and if you really don't get along, you can decide not to interact. At work, it's not a choice – your bills depend on your sociability.

So, as you can imagine, getting out of your corner to shed your shell and show off the fact that you are an interesting, energizing person can be hard.

Luckily, you don't need to put quite so much of yourself out there for your co-workers to analyse.

Here are some ways to show others just how reliable, powerful and knowledgeable you are—in order to earn the attention, and recognition you deserve:

Decide what it is you want. Being clear about what you want will allow you to stay focused on the prize—and stop at nothing to achieve it.

If you're still discovering what it is you want, creating a list of 30 things that you desire is a great way to start.

For about half an hour, ask yourself, "What do I want?" Don't censor yourself. It could be anything. It could be a house by the beach, the ability to set your own schedule, the ability to paint landscapes, or take pictures.

After you ask yourself what you want, spend about ten minutes asking yourself, what kind of person do I want to be?

You may find yourself with answers such as, "I want to be in a powerful position," or "I want a beautiful beach house in Florida," or "I want to have the time and creative freedom in a job that allows me to set my own schedule.

" By starting to answer the question of, "What do I want," and "what kind of person do I want to be," you can begin to dream big, broaden your reality, and begin the steps necessary to make your dreams come true.

Act if it you already have what it is you want. Acting 'as if' is an attraction principle that people have been using to receive promotions, and skyrocket their success to levels beyond what they even imagine.

If you want to become the owner of a company, but you haven't been able to stand out from the crowd, acting 'as if' you already have what you want is a great way to do it.

Acting 'as if' is all about asserting yourself with the traits a successful person (in the position you want) exudes on a daily basis.

Think about what a successful person acts like.

They aren't wishy-washy about the decisions they have to make to succeed in their job.

They don't come in late to work or leave early.

They don't look to others for validation.

They aren't insecure about the work they produce.

They actively pursue learning new skills in order to enhance their position of power. They dress for success. That's the kind of attitude and behavior you must exude.

When you do—by acting, dressing and looking the part, the 'as if' approach will pay off in getting you noticed and commanding that others respect and reward you for your devotion to your job.

Here are some more key points to keep in mind to make you more likable and recognizable in your office.

Body language—come in to work on time (with some time to spare, which is even better); have straight posture, give firm handshakes and dress for success.

Show interest in other people's needs and desires—be a team player, and contribute to the work place in a positive, helpful way.

Be proactive and willing to "own" your ideas—there's no such thing as a 'bad idea'. Every idea is an opportunity to learn, grow and thrive in a professional setting.

Don't avoid anyone – you may never know who will become your next ally.

Build skill sets in many areas—in order to remain competitive in your field, the key is continuing your own education. Take it upon yourself to read up on hone in on a new skill for three hours per week. Strengthen intellectual and/or creative 'muscles' you never knew you had!

Focus on stress reduction through meditation and positive thinking.

Set and keep goals regularly—short term goals will keep you on track, long term goals will keep you motivated and a reward system will allow you to continue the momentum of being a skilled goal setter!

To make sure you get the most out of your relationships, invest enough energy into displaying who you are to colleagues, then show them that the real you is valuable and best of all, likable.

Don't be demanding and always be willing to bend to accommodate (to a point). People will like you because of it, and more importantly they will *respec*t what you contribute as a person, and as a colleague.

Friends and Family

How do you maintain friendships and close relationships with your family using the tips we've outlined in this book?

By showing respect and building a relationship with everyone in your family.

When it comes to your friends, you'll want to make sure you're a good friend – someone who provides value to everyone you meet, who is empathetic to everyone's problems and who shows a 100% dedication to each moment you spend with them.

Key Points:

Empathy—facilitate a tighter bond than before by sympathizing and commiserating with their pleasure, or their pain.

Bond with them over the small things—as in romantic relationships, it's the small things in life that really mean the most. Having a cup of coffee together, spending time hanging out and talking about everything under the sun, or playing golf. It's about the moments inside your friendship that make it real, unique, and irreplaceable.

Avoid people who make you feel bad—life's too short to be around and/or accommodate others who don't lift you up.

Take and handle criticism as best as you can—no one's perfect, and that includes you. Friends talk about what's on their mind, and being a good friend means you can have an open mind and a healthy perspective when it comes to constructive feedback.

Focus on what you give to your friend's lives, rather than what you get. Come from a giving state in all of your relationships, instead of keeping tabs on what you're getting.

Friendship, more than anything else, is a huge part of the human experience.

We're hard wired to seek the approval and time of other people. We are meant to bond and to connect with others.

Enjoy your friendships and be willing to put as much of yourself as possible into every moment of them. By doing that, you'll be able to create a connection that lasts for a lifetime.

Impressing People

As human beings, we want to impress the people we meet from day to day.

Your partner's parents, the new boss at work, and that prospective new partner sitting across from you at the bar all have an impact on your life.

Did you know that what you see is only half of what is really there?

Did you know that what you hear is only half of what is really there?

Why does the mind work like this?

It's because so much is going on in your environment that the mind has to create this *Reality Distortion Field* in order to process what is going on...

...And your mind has to give you its best guess based on little psychological shortcuts that it uses based on thousands of years of evolution and also from experiences throughout your life.

So how can you use this *Reality Distortion Field* to your advantage?

Well, when we make decisions, there are mindless compliance psychological shortcuts at work, which save us time and enable us to make decisions without spending hours and hours deliberating over each and every decision (you of course get to learn about many of these in this book.)

But what I want to focus on in this chapter is what many have coined the *Reality Distortion Field*.

It was first called this by Bud Tripple from Apple, to describe Apples co-founder Steve Jobs charisma and its effects on the developers working on the Macintosh project. If you know how to use it properly, the *Reality Distortion Field* that you can create is said to distort your

audience's sense of proportion and scales of difficulties to them believe that the task at hand is possible...

...And this is really important if you want to be able to convince people to take on a seemingly difficult project.

In the case of Apple, Steve Jobs used the Reality Distortion Field technique by combining charisma, marketing, persistence and appeasement.

In dating, some people use it to convince their friends that they can get a certain person to go out with them, regardless of how challenging it might at first seem (yet these are the reasons why some people end up with someone outside of their league.

People who harness a reality distortion field are seen to be charismatic, leaders and people who make the impossible, possible. Whether or not they end up making their goal of the impossible, possible, it's not really the point.

These people who use this technique are so charismatic, that people of all ages, nationalities and races are drawn to them like a moth to a flame, and sucked into their reality.

In other words, the promise of what they are going to be delivered doesn't matter so much as how they feel in the moment—and with those who used the reality distortion field, they make them feel loved, validated, energized.

It's not a complicated technique, and anyone can do it with some practice coming across confident, self-assured and trustworthy.

Easily impress people by understanding what it is they want (a cheaper deal, a loving relationship, a better car) and talk from your own experience of having what they have. Then make it seem easier than they ever think it could be.

Remember earlier in this book how I discussed the importance of coming across as an expert.

Deep down, most people are insecure, unsure and fearful of change—so they never change. Instead, they complain about what they don't have, or maybe hope for change at best.

However, hope is a begger. It doesn't produce results.

On the other hand, when you can communicate with others that you have what they want—and that it was easier to get than you ever thought it would be—then you've already impressed 99 percent of your audience.

You've changed their perception of *what could be*, and brought them into your reality. Now all that's left is applying the body language tricks, confidence boosters and mindset secrets you've read about in this book!

Impressing people shouldn't be a selective activity.

You should work to provide as much interest and value as possible to every man, woman and child you know. These are people who have an impact on your life.

They help you solve problems, provide insights into your life, and generally make sure you feel good about yourself from day to day. They should be the first and foremost on our list of people to impress.

Jobs come and go.

People come and go.

Experiences come and go.

But, your friends, family and loved ones will be there for the rest of your life and they deserve the same treatment as anyone you meet on the street corner or in a bar.

Remember that and I guarantee you'll be one of the most likable people anyone in your circle will ever know.

Final Thoughts

"Charisma is not so much about getting people to like you as getting people to like themselves when you're around."

– Robert Brault

Becoming a well-liked people magnet is a skill, yes some people tend to be more natural than others and it can sometimes look like it's something that you're born with... But it isn't.

I've seen, not just from myself, but from hundreds of others whom I've helped with my methods that this can be learned just like any other skill.

But also, just like any other skill (e.g. learning guitar, learning a foreign language, or getting better at sport), it takes 3 critical steps...

Understanding what you need to be doing

Practice and doing what it takes to train your subconscious to take on the Auto Magnetism belief system

Using it in real life. Sometimes new things can feel slightly uncomfortable at first, just like a new technique at swinging a tennis racquet, but often times the greatest things in life are just outside your comfort zone, so just remember that it isn't necessarily supposed to feel comfortable or normal till you've done things many times.

There are many important belief systems to imprint in your mind, and we've covered a whole heap of them in this book.

I hope you have enjoyed and gained great value from this Book.

All the Best

9 781790 870363